"Have you seen a book in whose title appears the word *justice* and then you read, from start to finish, and it is just about compassion? This is not one of them! I commend *Call for Justice: From Practice to Theory and Back* to all, but more importantly to: teachers and preachers, because this book is a corrective to distortions of the gospel that are dominant on the Christian landscape; leaders and workers in Christian-based organizations in compassion, development, and justice work, because your understanding and practice will be enriched; to activists for justice, because you will be encouraged to keep hope. It is a powerful book! Simple and yet profound!"

—Bishop David Zac Niringiye, Senior Fellow with the
Institute for Religion, Faith, and Culture in Public Life in Uganda,
Visiting Fellow at Fuller Theological Seminary, and author of
The Church: God's Pilgrim People

"Ver Beek and Wolterstorff bring the fullness of their friendship to a rich analysis of faith, social justice, and advocacy. Whether you want to learn more about how change is brought to Honduras, or how social justice is seen through the prism of faith, *Call for Justice: From Practice to Theory and Back* is worthy of your time."

—Ali Noorani, Executive Director of the National Immigration Forum and
author of *There Goes the Neighborhood*

"In *Call to Justice*, the authors display something exceptional: a model of doing justice that bridges today's best justice theory with the vanguard of justice practice. *Call to Justice* is a field guide for anyone committed to pursuing deep and lasting change. Those brave enough to accept its invitation, and tenacious enough to endure the long haul, will experience the kind of breakthroughs we long for."

—Stephan Bauman, author of *Break Open the Sky* and *Seeking Refuge*

"This book is about how tenacity, bravery, and commitment can deal with the devastating impact of corruption. It emphasizes the often overlooked importance of hope as a driver to initiate and sustain action. Without hope, cynicism prevails along with inertia."

—Huguette Labelle, Former Chair of Transparency International

"In recent years, a growing number of Christians have recognized the centrality of justice to the biblical narrative. Often, though, justice can feel like an abstract concept: what does it look like in real life to follow the biblical injunction to seek justice? Nicholas Wolterstorff and Kurt Ver Beek—a Christian philosopher and a practitioner based at the Asociación para una Sociedad más Justa in Honduras, respectively—have offered a tremendous service to the global church by allowing us to eavesdrop on their conversations in *Call for Justice: From Practice to Theory and Back*. Rooted both in Scripture and in the practical experience of brave Christians working against violence and corruption in Honduras, this is a book that the church needs."

—Matthew Soerens, U.S. Director of Church Mobilization, World Relief
and co-author of *Seeking Refuge: On the Shores of the Global Refugee Crisis*

"Kurt and Nick invite us into an extensive exchange of ideas about what social justice means and how to achieve it. Kurt is a powerful storyteller—his stories of injustices suffered by the poor are shocking and heart wrenching, but the individual resolutions and systemic solutions achieved by ASJ for the poor are truly inspirational and highly relevant to all of us working to improve the lives of the poor."

—John Wingle, Honduras Country Director,
Millennium Challenge Corporation

"*Call for Justice: From Practice to Theory and Back* demonstrates how people of faith are engaging in the messy space of social justice advocacy and changing unjust systems. ASJ's extraordinary experience of seeking justice in Honduras proves that loving our neighbor means pursuing accountability for rampant impunity and corruption in our midst. *Call for Justice* offers concrete examples of how corrupt political systems and unbridled power prevent human flourishing, but at the same time it shares what brave hope and action for change looks like. This rich dialogue between a philosopher and a practitioner includes topics from coalition building to restorative justice, and orients us on what it takes to honor the God given dignity of every person and to transform systemic injustices of our time."

—Krisanne Vaillancourt Murphy, Executive Director,
Catholic Mobilizing Network and co-author of *Advocating for Justice:
An Evangelical Vision for Transforming Systems and Structures*

"If you are a pastor, a professor, or a committed advocate for justice, this is an essential book that equips and convicts. Churches and classrooms will find this accessible philosophically with case-studies that make the philosophy and action come to life. Deep. Inviting. Authentic."

—Shirley Hoogstra, President, Council for Christian Colleges & Universities

"For followers of Jesus motivated to deepen their understanding of doing justice, *Call for Justice* is now the best place to start. This rich conversation between two friends blends wise, inspiring stories of ASJ's best practices in Honduras with a potent distillation of Wolterstorff's seminal work in the philosophy of justice. The result is a compelling vision for how theory and practice should sharpen each other as we seek to bravely embody biblical justice."

—Gary VanderPol, co-author of *Return to Justice* and
senior pastor, Church Without Walls

"Kurt Ver Beek and the ASJ team have dedicated themselves to the work of justice in Honduras with relentless courage and tenacity. For decades ASJ has defended and protected the vulnerable, even in the face of violent opposition. As an exploration of the ASJ model for transforming justice systems, *Call for Justice* embodies a rare combination of warmth and rigor; it's highly accessible as a dialogue between Ver Beek and Wolterstorff, while also providing a framework for confronting corruption and engaging broken justice systems. This book will be a significant companion for anyone who is serious about doing the work of justice over the long haul."

—Gary A. Haugen, CEO, International Justice Mission

"I am struck by the intrinsic power of the authors' use of letters for their higher order reflections on social justice. The dialogical learning that this exchange enables is transformative and models the importance of reciprocity for theorists and practitioners as they link ideas and action. The modesty and humility present in the letters inspires all who take seriously the importance of dialogue as a means for reflection and practice of social justice in our communities."

—Ivy George, Professor of Sociology, Gordon College

"If you have ever called for justice to be done, but never engaged in the messy, complex, and perilous work of practical reform, then this book is for you. If you seek to bring about justice by the work of your hands each day, but struggle to articulate the reasoning that motivates your work, then this book is for you. Kurt Ver Beek and Nicholas Wolterstorff have produced an excellent work that bridges theory and practice, ideas and consequences, and the yearning for justice in the broken systems that so often cripple human flourishing. The authors help us to see that when we do the work of justice, we also put our trust in the slow work of God. All readers will find a challenge embedded in this work: nuance and complexity for the idealist; moral aspiration for the realist; and great hope for the cynic."

—Michael Le Roy, President, Calvin University

"*Call for Justice: From Practice to Theory and Back* struck me as a remarkable book in a number of ways. The book uses a clever literary device—an exchange of letters between philosopher Nicholas Wolterstorff and activist Kurt Ver Beek—to bridge the gap between the theory and practice of justice. Both authors are muscular Christians who bring deep faith to courageous activism. You'll learn a lot about the differences between development, relief, and justice; about political, prophetic, and priestly authorities; about how governments fail their citizens; and how justice is the most important thing to those abandoned by society."

—James D. Nealon, Former US Ambassador to Honduras 2014–2017

Call for Justice

FROM PRACTICE
TO THEORY
AND BACK

~~~~~~~~~~~

Kurt Ver Beek *and* Nicholas P. Wolterstorff

Foreword by Ruth Padilla DeBorst

CASCADE *Books* · Eugene, Oregon

CALL FOR JUSTICE
From Practice to Theory and Back

Cascade Books
An Imprint of Wipf and Stock Publishers
199 W. 8th Ave., Suite 3
Eugene, OR 97401

www.wipfandstock.com

PAPERBACK ISBN: 978-1-5326-9219-2
HARDCOVER ISBN: 978-1-5326-9220-8
EBOOK ISBN: 978-1-5326-9221-5

Cataloguing-in-Publication data:

Names: Ver Beek, Kurt, author. | Wolterstorff, Nicholas, author.
Title: Call for justice : from practice to theory and back again / Kurt Ver Beek and Nicholas Wolterstorff.
Description: Eugene, OR: Cascade Books, 2019 | Includes bibliographical references.
Identifiers: ISBN 978-1-5326-9219-2 (paperback) | ISBN 978-1-5326-9220-8 (hardcover) | ISBN 978-1-5326-9221-5 (ebook)
Subjects: LCSH: Christianity and Justice. | Justice (Philosophy). | Human rights—Religious aspects—Christianity. | Justice, Administration of—Honduras.
Classification: BV4639 .C256 2019 (paperback) | BV4639 (ebook)

Manufactured in the U.S.A.   11/05/19

CONTENTS

PART 2

JUSTICE, LOVE, AND FORGIVENESS

PART 3

JUSTICE, COALITIONS, AND KEEPING THE VISION ALIVE

PART 4

ASJ AS A CHRISTIAN ORGANIZATION

FOREWORD

His was a conversion. A deep, broad, life-transformative conversion. One that would not have been possible if he had not
stepped out of his bubble, out of the comfort zone of his familiar
world. You know what bubbles are like. We all live comfortably in
them and they determine what we see, how we see, who we see—
and who or what we don't! And these bubbles tend to calcify; they
become impervious to winds of change and turn our worlds into
echo chambers in which all we hear are resonances of our preexist-
ing perspectives.

Sidney Rooy, a Dutch American missionary, church historian,
and devoted member of the Latin American Theological Fellowship,
loves to share the conversion he underwent when he first read the
Bible in Spanish. While in English translations the Hebrew words
sedeq and *mispat* are most often rendered as "righteousness"—a term
which in the mind of most people describes a personal moral condition linking an individual properly with God—those same words
are translated in Spanish Bibles as *"justicia"*. Many other languages
similarly translate these words with terms equivalent to "justice"
and therefore point toward God's call for a much broader mending
of what has been broken at all levels of society. Take, for example,
Isaiah 32:17 and ponder the difference *justicia* brings to this text that
in English appears to point to a very individual condition:

> The fruit of that righteousness will be peace;
> its effect will be quietness and confidence forever.

Now replace "righteousness" with "justice" and note how the entire scenario broadens. Justice, which is social, economic, and ecological, is now a prerequisite for full-orbed peace! A whole new horizon opened up for this missionary as he read the Old Testament through an entirely new lens while living alongside people who were suffering from the impact of dictatorships, military interventions, poverty, and inequality. His comfortable, somewhat calcified bubble was cracked open. He saw difficult realities to which he had previously remained blind. He heard voices to which he had previously remained deaf. His understanding was radically expanded regarding the calling of God's people in God's world. Sidney Rooy became a prophetic voice and an activist for justice for the rest of his life.

The rich conversation into which Call for Justice invites us both illustrates and invites readers into similar conversions, eye-opening and ear-unstopping conversions. The authors weave together their experiences, the biblical and contextual explorations, and the troubling quandaries each of them (and their communities) bring to the task of doing the work of justice. Each in their own way struggles to live in a broken world as representatives of the divine Creative-Community-of-Love in light of God's good purposes for the entire creation. The unique and provocative gift of this letter exchange between Kurt and Nick is their honest probing for depth and their authentic account of their journey of conversion to justice. Kurt reflects on how he and his wife, Jo Ann, stepped beyond the paradigm of "development" into the messy complexity of deep justice work along with Carlos Hernández and other Hondurans of ASJ. Nick expresses how his ethical formulations were stretched by the front-line challenges faced by sisters and brothers from places very different than his own backyard, and particularly by the work of the Asociación para una Sociedad más Justa.

Undoubtedly, the book you have in your hands will certainly serve as a generative handbook for justice work, with unique insights and road-tested practices and insights. At the same time, if you allow God's Spirit to crack open your calcified bubble, this candid exchange between the Christian philosopher and the Christian justice worker will surely discomfort you and prompt the needed conversions. It is my suspicion that, if previous generations of Christians needed to broaden their understanding and practice of the good news of Jesus Christ to include social justice, current generations need to deepen their understanding further by transcending the faddish modes of "virtual" adherence to causes. Justice cannot be pursued by remote control. As Kurt and Nick so graphically display, justice work is dangerous and costly. If it is to yield lasting transformation, it must move beyond denunciation to the long hard slog of embodied, full-life, long-term commitment to people in tough places and to the God whose purposes are for full life for all people. It involves negotiation and respectful partnerships—across borders of all sorts—responsible research, clear communication, naming injustice, granting and receiving forgiveness, surrendering control, and persevering in hope that God has not given up on God's world.

My husband James and I have been privileged to count Kurt and Jo Ann, Nick and his wife Claire, among our treasured friends and inspirers for many decades. Neither that familiarity nor my background as a woman born and raised in lands that have been on the receiving end of colonial enterprises since Europeans "discovered" them, however, exonerates me from facing my own need for ongoing conversion. Invited as I am to speak about justice, I run the terrible risk of pointing my finger at the passivity of others, varnishing my bubble with platitudes, and becoming ever more disengaged from the injustices in my own community. How might I—and you—avoid those pitfalls? Well, Sidney Rooy was converted to justice by reading Scripture in Spanish and seeing reality afresh thanks to the friendship with people from outside his cultural and linguistic circle, outside of his bubble. No doubt Kurt and Nick can attest to how the intentional exchange between them has enriched their search for God's justice in the world. So for all Christians the step of crossing respectfully into the world of others, those different from ourselves, can silence our ready-made answers that we may hear the small, still voice of the Spirit of wisdom and understanding, of knowledge and fear of the Lord (Isaiah 11:2) and then to follow in the footsteps of our Lord. May it be so!

RUTH PADILLA DEBORST
Latin American Theological Fellowship

ACKNOWLEDGMENTS

Acknowledgments—Joint

To Pete Harkema, who first suggested
that we do a book together about ASJ.

To Jill Stoltzfus, who persistently prodded us to keep working at it.

And finally and most gratefully, to Kate Parsons, who with her deep
understanding of ASJ, her passion for justice, and her exceptional writing and
editing skills, helped us to think more deeply and articulate more clearly the
stories and ideas in this book. By working and reworking draft after draft
and patiently keeping the two of us on task, Kate helped us craft this
book out of our sometimes disorderly exchange of letters and ideas.
GRACIAS!

Acknowledgments—Nick

Claire Kingma Wolterstorff, who, with her passion for the demeaned and
downtrodden, has been my companion these many years on the journey
toward a more just society and who enthusiastically supported the
writing of these letters.

Acknowledgments—Kurt

Carlos Hernandez and Jo Ann Van Engen.
The work of ASJ described in this book is the product of countless
passionate conversations with these two co-conspirators.

ABOUT THIS BOOK

This book is an exchange of letters that highlights the work of the Asociación para una Sociedad más Justa, or ASJ, a Honduran organization based in Tegucigalpa, Honduras. Coauthor Kurt Ver Beek and a group of his Honduran friends founded ASJ in 1998 with the goal of being brave Christians who try to make government systems work better and more justly for the most vulnerable of Honduran society.

A few years later, Kurt and a group of his North American friends founded the US-based Association for a more Just Society (AJS), with the goal of supporting ASJ's work in Honduras as well as inspiring others around the world to seek justice in their own contexts.

PROLOGUE

Kurt Ver Beek and I had known each other in a casual sort of way for a good many years. Then, beginning around fifteen years ago, whenever he was in Grand Rapids for a few weeks in the summer, he would call me up at my home there and suggest that we get together for coffee. After catching up on news about our families and mutual friends, and after sharing some details of what we had been doing the past year, Kurt would tell me about the current projects of the organization in Honduras that he had helped to found and of which he was co-director, the Asociación para una Sociedad más Justa, or ASJ.

And then, each time, as we were about to part ways, he would bring up the same topic: how about my flying down to Tegucigalpa to observe firsthand the work of ASJ? He had been following what I had been writing about justice, he knew of my support for a number of justice movements and organizations in the US and elsewhere, and he was confident that I would find firsthand observation of what ASJ was doing a significant addition to my experience.

For several years I pleaded the press of other obligations. Finally, in March 2010, there was an opening in my schedule, and I flew down to Tegucigalpa. "Awed" is not too strong a word for what I saw and heard about the work of ASJ. I had participated in the American civil rights movement and in the opposition to the Vietnam War, I had been a close observer of the anti-apartheid movement in South Africa, and I had been chair of the board of a US organization concerned with justice for the Palestinians, Palestine Human Rights Campaign. So I was well acquainted with social justice movements and orga-

I

nizations. But in addressing itself to the particularities of the situation in Honduras, ASJ had crafted strategies for combatting social injustice that I had not seen employed elsewhere. The imagination that went into devising those strategies, and the tenacity and bravery displayed in carrying them out, were awesome.

Upon returning home, I wrote an article for *The Christian Century* in which I described some of the distinctive ways in which ASJ was working for social justice in Honduras, and formulated what I saw as the rationale for working in those ways. The response of Kurt and others in ASJ to the article was that I had put into words what they recognized to be implicit in what they were doing, but which they themselves had never made explicit, and that this would, they were sure, prove valuable for guiding their actions in the future.

After that initial visit to Honduras, I subsequently flew down to Tegucigalpa on three other occasions to observe the work of ASJ. Each time, my observations, along with conversations with Kurt and other members of the staff of ASJ, gave me additional insight into how ASJ operated and why it had settled on operating as it did.

From those conversations the idea emerged of the two of us together writing a book in which we would describe some of the distinctive features of how ASJ operates and would elicit the principles, explicit and implicit, behind operating in that way. We judged that a book presenting this interplay between practice and theory would not only be of interest to those concerned with what was happening in Honduras but would also be suggestive and illuminating for those working for social justice in other parts of the world. ASJ would function as a case study of practices and principles that have application well beyond Honduras.

Fine idea! But how to do it? A jointly written book? Too laborious, especially when we are located thousands of miles away from each other, Kurt in Tegucigalpa and I in Grand Rapids, Michigan. How about an exchange of letters between Kurt, the activist, and me, the philosopher, with each of us feeling free to infringe, every now and then, on the territory of the other? That would be a way for us to continue our conversation and for others to listen in. So that's what this is, an exchange of letters on practices and principles of justice, with ASJ as our case study.

It's typical of lengthy letter exchanges that there are bumps along the way that one notices when one goes back to review the exchange: repetitions, questions asked that didn't get answered, one person ignoring the last letter from the other person and instead going back to a point he made in an earlier letter, etc. In editing these letters for publication, we have worked to eliminate such bumps; but it's likely we have missed some of them.

Let me add that exchanging these letters has been, for me, a learning experience. From Kurt's letters I have learned things about the workings of ASJ that I had not previously known, in spite of the fact that I have several times observed firsthand how ASJ works. And in eliciting the principles, implicit and explicit, that shape and guide how ASJ works, I have found myself reflecting on dimensions of justice, and of working for justice, that I had not previously thought about.

May 2019   NICHOLAS WOLTERSTORFF

PART 1

THE FOUNDING OF ASJ AND HOW IT WORKS

I

A First Letter

Dear Kurt,

On my initial visit to Honduras to observe firsthand the work of ASJ, I was both moved and struck by many things. We will get to them later. But what especially struck me was the fact that ASJ was very definitely a justice organization—not a relief or development organization. Of course, I should have realized that ASJ was a justice organization from the fact that "justice" is in its name. But it hadn't really sunk in—probably because most of the work that American Christians support overseas is either traditional mission work or relief or development work. Relatively little is devoted to social justice.

For me, the clearest indicator that ASJ was doing justice work was that what it was doing was dangerous—very dangerous. I learned that around five years earlier Dionisio Díaz García, a lawyer for ASJ, had been killed by two hit men on a motorcycle as he was headed for court.

A rather good rule of thumb is that if an organization is working to improve the condition of some segment of the populace and in doing so, stirs up hostility on the part of those who have something to lose, the work it is doing is probably justice work. That's because, when struggling to correct some injustice, one has to point fingers at those who are perpetrating the injustice, accuse them, and try to get them to stop. And they don't like being accused and don't want to stop—no surprise there! Relief and development work, while important and necessary, do not often result in threats of violence because they do not, as such, require pointing accusing fingers.

7

So here's my first question for you, Kurt: how did it happen that you co-founded a justice organization, and how did it happen that you co-founded the organization in Honduras? I have heard pieces of the story, but never the whole story. As I recall, your graduate school training was in development work, and you initially went to Honduras to work for a relief organization. If that is correct, what led you to start working for justice? And what led you to found ASJ?

Your friend,
Nick

2

The Founding of ASJ

Dear Nick,

I remember your first trip to Honduras very well. You may have left Honduras with a new sense of what justice work could look like, but our rich conversations during that week left me equally inspired. I felt you gave me new language to express the vision that ASJ had long been implementing.

The path that led to the organization that you saw in 2010, and in your subsequent trips, was not a clear one. I certainly never imagined the breadth or scope of work that we would be doing. Jo Ann and I moved to Honduras just months after we graduated from college, and for six years we worked in community development. Those were formative years for us—we were living alongside people in poverty, digging deeply into the culture and language, and learning about development, even if sometimes through trial and error. But the longer we worked on these health, agriculture, and microfinance projects, the more we felt something was missing. We wanted our work to help the most vulnerable people in Honduras, but increasingly we understood that their problems were deeper than training and loans could fix.

In the 1990s, I decided to get my PhD in Development Sociology at Cornell, and I was very focused on learning more about community development. When I graduated, Jo Ann and I wanted to start a practical, hands-on semester in Honduras for college students— teaching them all the things we wished we had known when we started working internationally. I remember several occasions when professors asked me if I wasn't more interested in looking at things from a structural level, and I always said no. We had loved our experience of community development and wanted to be with the people, in the community.

Even before I finished my doctorate, we sent a proposal for a semester in Honduras to a number of colleges. Calvin College, our alma mater, responded quickly and hired Jo Ann and me to start the program.

When our first group came down in 1996, we designed three course-sections for them. We started out teaching them everything we knew about Honduras—its history, culture, economics, and politics.

The second section was all about community development—both the most common problems a poor community faces, and practical solutions to alleviate those problems. I would draw a matrix on the board and together we would fill it in—what are the problems Honduras faces at a community level? What are some solutions? Which organizations are working on those solutions? We talked about local health and sanitation issues, education, agriculture, microenterprise—all the things on the community development palette at the time. Between the students and me, we always came up with dozens of organizations, both Christian and secular, that were working on those community development issues.

Our third course focused on national and international issues facing Honduras—immigration, debt, trade, violence, and government corruption. I would put the same matrix on the board, and again it was easy to think through problems, and even propose some solutions and their pros and cons. But when we got to the column identifying who was working in these areas, we couldn't think of any organizations doing this work. Even after my ten years in Honduras, I knew of very few organizations working on macro issues like violence and corruption, and almost none of them were Christian.

I gradually felt convicted. I knew that if I talked to my neighbors and asked them about their priorities, few of them would talk about microloans. The issues that kept them up at night were deeper. *Will the hospital have medicine for me? Will the gangs kill my son as they killed his father?* My neighbors' problems were not just the lack of some material good. The fragility of their lives was a direct effect of a government that was failing to protect its most vulnerable people.

Jo Ann and I decided to hold a meeting with some of our friends in Tegucigalpa in order to share a vision of an organization that would address some of these serious structural issues that Honduras faced. Four of our friends, all Honduran, decided to join us, and we ended that meeting by naming the first board of directors of La Asociación para una Sociedad más Justa, or ASJ. One of those founding members was Carlos Hernández, a young school principal and community leader. I didn't know him very well at the time, but he would soon become one of my best friends, and a lifelong partner in working for justice.

Those early years with ASJ felt a little bit like our first years in community development—a lot of trial and error. All of us on the board of directors chipped in to rent our first office—the garage behind someone's apartment—and we hired a friend part-time to help us figure out what we were going to do.

I'm proud of the victories we achieved in the first few years, such as helping communities get legal title to their homes and protecting the labor rights of vulnerable workers. But those victories felt at times like many different stabs at this nebulous "cloud" of injustice. One of our biggest goals was to expose corruption, something we thought would be relatively easy, because Honduran elites seemed to break and abuse laws so blatantly. We quickly learned it wasn't as easy as we thought.

One of our first big cases began when community leaders from a marginalized settlement came to us to report that they were being forced to buy their land twice—once from the city, and once from a lawyer who claimed that he was the rightful owner of the settlement land. After six months of searching through complex, unorganized property registrations, we were able to prove that the community was, in fact, situated on city land, and that the lawyer had no right to it. Convincing a judge of this would take many more months of tireless work. But though this work wasn't easy, we quickly learned how far-reaching a victory could be.

In the process of fighting for this one community, we were able not only to clear the way for more than 20,000 residents to get their land titles, but also to draft and help pass legislation that would change the way all land disputes in Honduras were settled—thereby helping to protect hundreds of thousands of poor Hondurans whose homes were threatened by unscrupulous opportunists. The diligence and activism of our staff resulted in government systems working better, which, in turn, affected lives across the entire country.

As we began to see these results, the purpose of ASJ as a "justice organization" really began to crystalize. Our work in education wouldn't just focus on a few schools; it would target the Ministry of Education who administered over 22,000 schools. Our work in health wouldn't focus on local clinics or medical brigades; it would analyze the multimillion-dollar medicines budget being mishandled by the Ministry of Health. Even our work in community violence wasn't intended just to lower homicide rates in our target communities but to model for the rest of the country what effective violence prevention could look like.

Twenty years later, Jo Ann and I still run our study-abroad program every year, and we still try to teach students all the things we wish we had known when we started doing this work. We teach them that systemic problems require a systemic solution. We teach them that development work needs to intersect with justice work, challenging inequalities and injustices built into government and legal systems. And when we draw those matrices, showing who's working in those areas, I'm pleased that ASJ makes that list.

Thinking about how ASJ started makes me wonder about your own interest in justice. You have spent much of your life pursuing justice in practice, and much of your academic career thinking and writing about justice; your reflections on the philosophical and spiritual nature of justice span several books. With all the lines of inquiry open to a philosopher, what led you to think and write about justice, particularly the Christian approach to justice?

Your friend,
Kurt

3

Apartheid and Palestine:
Awakening to the Call for Social Justice

Dear Kurt,

That was a very interesting letter, spelling out how you got interested in justice issues in Honduras and why it was that you and others founded ASJ. What you write suggests a number of questions that I would like to put to you. But before we get to those, I'll answer your question as to how I, a philosopher, got interested in issues of social justice.

It happened quite differently from how it happened in your case. In your case, it happened in a classroom: you and your students identified a certain range of issues facing Honduras—issues of social justice, as it turned out, though I would guess that you did not immediately identify them as such—and then came to the realization that there were almost no organizations working on those issues. In my case, it happened by being confronted, unexpectedly, with victims of injustice and hearing their cry for justice.

In the '60s and early '70s I was a vocal supporter of the civil rights movement and a vocal opponent of the Vietnam War. A few years ago, I looked over some of the things I had written at the time and some of the notes I had preserved for speeches I gave, and noticed that they referred, every now and then, to justice. So justice was present in my thinking and writing. But it was not prominent; it was not on my agenda.

Then, in September 1975, the college where I was a young professor in the philosophy department, Calvin College, sent me to represent the college at a conference at the University of Potchefstroom in

Potchefstroom, South Africa. Potchefstroom is a city of medium size not far from Johannesburg. At the time, the university did not enroll black students. The topic of the conference was Christian higher education around the world in the tradition of Reformed Protestantism. There were a good many Afrikaners present at the conference, along with a fair number of so-called black and colored scholars from South Africa. (I am using the terms "black" and "colored" as they were used at the time in South Africa.) There was a sizable contingent of Dutch scholars present, a few from other parts of Africa and from Asia, and a few of us from the US and Canada.

In 1975, apartheid was still in full force in South Africa. Though apartheid was not the topic of the conference, it was the main topic of conversation in coffee breaks and at meals. And the Dutch, who were very well informed about apartheid and very angry at the Afrikaner regime, managed to intrude the issue of apartheid into the conference itself in the form of sly questions that they asked in the question periods after lectures. After a few days of this, the Afrikaners, thoroughly exasperated at the Dutch for hijacking their conference, agreed to hold an evening session devoted specifically to the topic of apartheid. It remains one of the most intense discussions I have ever been part of.

The Dutch vented their anger at the Afrikaner regime for the system of apartheid. I later learned that Afrikaners typically responded to criticisms of apartheid by insisting that the critics were ignorant of crucial facts. They could not accuse the Dutch of ignorance; the Dutch were obviously very well informed. So, instead, the Afrikaners who spoke up in that evening session charged the Dutch with arrogant judgmentalism. The Dutch did not accept this criticism lying down!

After maybe forty-five minutes of intense back and forth, neither party had anything new to say to the other. It was then that the South Africans of color began to speak up. They described in moving detail the oppression and indignities to which they were systematically subjected by apartheid, and they issued a ringing call for justice. Not only was I deeply moved; the conviction washed over me that, by way of their call for justice, God was calling me to speak up with and for these suffering people. I would be religiously disobedient if I did not.

The response by the Afrikaners speaking up in defense of apartheid to this call for justice took me completely aback. Justice, they said, was not the issue. Benevolence was the issue. They, the Afrikaners, were a generous people. The speakers explained that in South Africa there were ten or so different nationalities. The aim of apartheid was that each of these nationalities be enabled and encouraged to develop separately: develop their own microeconomies, develop their own style of basket-weaving, their own literature, etc. If this was to happen, they could not live mingled through each other. They had to be separated, hence, *apartheid*. Some of the speakers went on to describe acts of personal kindness on their part to so-called blacks and coloreds: clothing their own children had outgrown that they gave to the family living in their back yard, small gifts at Christmas, etc.

Then they went on the offensive against those who had spoken up against apartheid: why do you never express gratitude for what we do for you? Why do you only criticize us? "Why can't we just love each other," one asked, tears in her eyes. Never before had I so clearly seen the difference between benevolence and justice, and the importance of justice. Benevolence was being used as an instrument of oppression—*self-perceived* benevolence, of course.

I left South Africa a changed person. I had experienced an awakening; justice was on my agenda. I got myself informed about what was going on in South Africa, spoke and wrote extensively against apartheid, and began to think about justice more generally. I returned to South Africa several times over the next couple of decades.

A second awakening occurred two and a half years later. In May 1978 I attended a conference in Chicago on Palestinian rights. The conference was sponsored by an organization I had never previously heard of, the Palestine Human Rights Campaign. I never learned why I was invited, nor did I understand what it was in me that led me to attend. Along with everybody else that I knew, I had cheered Israel's victory in the 1967 war.

There were about 150 Palestinians at the conference. They poured out their hearts in flaming rhetoric, telling of the indignities daily heaped upon them by the Israeli occupation, and issuing a ringing call for justice. Not only was I deeply moved by this new call for justice; once again, the conviction washed over me that I was being issued a call from God to speak up with and for these suffering people.

I became informed about the situation in Israel-Palestine and its historical background, I became chair of the board of the Palestine Human Rights Campaign, and I spoke and wrote often in defense of the Palestinian cause. Over the next couple of decades I visited Israel-Palestine and the surrounding countries several times.

So there you have it, Kurt, that's how social justice got to me. It's not a cause I chose; it chose me. In your case, it seems that it was not just social justice that you committed yourself to, but Honduras itself. I imagine that working for social justice in a country that is not your native country has posed unique challenges to you. But I don't recall that we have ever talked about what it has meant to be a foreigner doing the sort of work that you do. Would you be willing to tell me a bit about that?

Your friend,
Nick

4

The Role of Foreigners in the Work of ASJ

Dear Nick,

Thanks for your letter describing what awakened your own concern for justice. It's striking to me that in the two episodes you describe, what happened is that you heard directly the victims of injustice. The same thing happened to Jo Ann and me; we heard directly from our Honduran neighbors who were suffering.

The question of my role as a foreigner in this country is one I have thought about a lot. ASJ is focused on securing justice in Honduras, and almost all of its staff are native Hondurans, including its co-director, Carlos. But I'm a foreigner; and though I have lived in Honduras for thirty-two years—longer than I have lived in the United States—I still sometimes grapple with what it means to be a foreigner here, particularly one in a position of leadership. However, over the last five years or so I have become more comfortable with my role here and with how I operate and present myself.

In some ways, I have come a long way since Jo Ann's and my first years in Honduras three decades ago. When we first arrived, we were barely twenty-two years old. Our Spanish wasn't great. We were recent college graduates with a shallow understanding of the local culture and what it took to really help the poor—we had no experience in international development. Nonetheless, for our first six years in the country we worked diligently as the representatives of a US-based development organization and were responsible for distributing $300,000 among six Honduran NGOs.

We certainly tried hard. We threw ourselves headfirst into learning Spanish, and were intentional about understanding and listening to the people around us. But it was often very uncomfortable. I know we made some bad decisions in those first few years, and stepped on a lot of toes.

Our experience is not an anomaly. US organizations send wide-eyed and well-intentioned North Americans into positions of leadership around the world. As someone who has been in this position, and who has interacted with many others in similar positions, this has come to bother me.

To express this discomfort, I often give the following example: if my son has a serious health issue, I don't want him being seen by a well-meaning pre-med student who barely speaks his language. I want someone with years of training and experience to examine him, someone who has seen many cases like his, and whom I can trust to lead him through the best treatment path possible.

In our communities and churches, we understand this desire for experience when it affects the people and things closest to us, but somehow, when it comes to helping the poor in another country (or even in our own inner cities, which for some suburban churches might as well be another country), we think it's acceptable to send people who have all the right motivations but little of the experience or cultural understanding that would help them do their job well.

Another troubling trend I have seen is the shift in US churches from supporting long-term missionaries and development workers to sending short-term mission groups who have even less contextual understanding, language ability, or relevant experience. These groups typically spend a week in a new country, leading Bible studies or building houses or schools. Volunteers on these trips speak of how meaningful the trips were to them personally, but I am skeptical of how effective they are as a form of development. Would these short-term mission volunteers want their own children to attend school in classrooms built by high schoolers with no construction experience? Would they allow one of their own babies to be delivered by a student in her second year of nursing school? The answer, of course, is no. Yet, by and large, we feel these interventions are appropriate when they occur in other countries.

Let me make clear that I am not against sending North Americans abroad, but I do believe that, for interventions to be successful, they require the leadership of qualified people who have the experience and cultural knowledge necessary to navigate the challenges of working in a developing country. Almost always, I have found, that leadership should be local. This leadership is particularly important when considering the imbalances of power that money and position generally bring. A Honduran brick layer will understand local construction requirements, land titling and permission regulations, and how houses should be built to withstand the heavy rains and mudslides in the region. But if his work is directed and paid for by a US group with a specific idea of how the resulting houses should look, that brick layer may not feel comfortable challenging those expectations.

It took Jo Ann and me a few years to get to a point where we really understood this power dynamic. During our first years in Honduras, things often went the way we wanted them to go; but it's clear to me now that while sometimes we may have had good insight or ideas, in other instances things went our way simply because of the resources and influence that went along with our positions. Looking back, I think we did the best we could with our lack of training and preparation. If I were to do it again, however, I would want to work for a few years under someone else, gaining experience and cultural context before we were put in charge.

In 1998, after Jo Ann and I had been working in Honduras for more than a decade, we joined Carlos Hernández and three other Hondurans to found ASJ. In these early years, Carlos was working full-time at a second job, while my job as a college professor gave me more flexibility; and so, in spite of the fact that we were running the organization together, it was frequently I who was calling press conferences or attending meetings with government officials.

Being a foreigner definitely had its advantages. I know that I sometimes got appointments with government officials or international organizations that Carlos would not have gotten. I was frequently treated with more respect, and there was less risk of violence against me or my family. Nonetheless, whenever I was called to speak for ASJ, there was often confusion: why was a North American leading a Honduran NGO? People would whisper about undue influence from the US government, or wonder about my motivations.

At this point, Jo Ann and I had made our lives in Honduras. By then, I had years of experience, I had earned a PhD, was fluent in Spanish, and was very familiar with Honduran culture. In spite of all that, I wasn't seen as Honduran, and any statement I made was judged not only on its content but on my identity.

Though my foreign name and face helped ASJ get its foot in the door on multiple occasions, when fierce conflicts flared up it was clear that my visibility was more a liability than an asset. As ASJ brought forward major problems such as access to running water, or the abysmal treatment of security guards and cleaning women, those responsible would be quick to respond that I, a foreigner, had no right to bring up these issues, or to publicly accuse them of such serious wrongdoing.

I don't think this is unusual. If, for example, a Chinese citizen formed an NGO in Chicago and began offering friendly advice to the mayor about how to address violence in Chicago communities, her input might be seen as interesting and worth considering; but the moment she began to publicly criticize and organize protest groups, the reception would turn chilly. Attention would turn not to the issues she was highlighting but to how inappropriate it was for her, a foreigner, to speak out about Chicago and its problems.

Thankfully, as ASJ grew, Carlos was eventually able to quit his second job and commit his time fully to ASJ. By then we had also hired a team of very capable Honduran leaders, and I was able to take on more of a background leadership position. Since then, we have been able to operate more in line with our individual gifts. Carlos and I work well together, not because we are Honduran and North American, but because we are two people with a shared vision and complementary skill sets. Over twenty years of working together we have struck a balance that allows us to lead a very effective organization.

In 2014, civil society leader Omar Rivera joined our team. He and Carlos are fabulous at press conferences and politically difficult meetings. They are gifted at presenting our message pointedly and consistently in private meetings, on television, and before very different groups of people.

My gifts are different. While Carlos and Omar are ASJ's public face, I work behind the scenes supervising our 150 staff members, designing and overseeing new research initiatives, and helping with the creation and monitoring of new programs that confront injustice. In the end, my "foreignness" is one of my gifts—not my only gift, and I hope not the most important, but one that allows me to position myself as a bridge builder between Honduras and the United States or English-speaking Europe. I can also generate attention, both within and outside of Honduras, that a Honduran leader would not be able to, and bring in strategic connections from the United States.

My role in AJS, the Association for a more Just Society (ASJ's sister organization in the United States), is much more straightforward. The role of AJS is to support the work of ASJ in Honduras and to do justice education. As a North American I am well-suited to that task. I regularly meet with individuals and foundations who wish to financially support ASJ and I speak regularly all over the US about what it means to do justice in a local context.

I am happy that leadership of ASJ lies with Carlos, Omar, and the other skilled Honduran leaders within ASJ, not only because they are so good at what they do, which they are, but also because I believe it is important for Hondurans to lead change in Honduras. They instinctively grasp the nuance in what people say or leave unsaid, they understand Honduras' history and how it affects the present, and this makes them much more effective in difficult meetings and conversations. I think their position as the face of ASJ also gives other Hondurans hope. It shows that you don't need to be foreign to lead change.

I feel privileged to work alongside my Honduran colleagues, and I am grateful for the chance to use my gifts to support their work. The "gift" of being North American, like all gifts, is one I try to use carefully and with humility. I understand that this gift is accompanied by privilege and power, and I try as best I can to use that power only in ways that build up and support my colleagues and their work.

I would not say that foreigners can never be in positions of influence in a place that is not their home; but anytime they represent a historically dominant culture—whether that is a North American in Honduras or a white leader in a predominantly Hispanic community in the US—their power should be acknowledged and balanced by joining voices with other people, acting with humility, and making decisions in consultation with people who have been there longer than they have.

Now I have a question for you. As you know, our work in Honduras involves working with the government, which is not an easy task. No country in the world has a completely transparent or effective government; and sometimes it seems that government systems do more harm than good. I am curious how you as a philosopher, and particularly as a Christian philosopher, would conceptualize the role of government in society. How do you understand the way we should think about government?

Your friend,
Kurt

5

A Scriptural View of the Task of Government

Dear Kurt,

Thanks for those reflections on the role of foreigners in social justice work. I admire your keen awareness of the potential obstacles of your foreignness while nonetheless remaining convinced that there is an appropriate role for you to play in Honduras, especially in working to improve the Honduran government.

As you know, one of the things that especially impressed me about the work of ASJ, when I first observed it, was precisely the relationship of ASJ to the Honduran government. Many organizations, including Christian organizations, when working in situations of serious injustice, content themselves with either alleviating the suffering, issuing denunciations of the government, or doing an end run around the government by setting up alternative institutions— alternative schools, alternative medical facilities, and the like. ASJ was doing something distinctly different, namely, trying to get the Honduran government to do what government is supposed to do. And that brings me to the question you put to me at the end of your letter: what is it that government is supposed to do? I take my bearings on this matter from Christian Scripture.

But before we get to what Scripture says about the task of government, I think it's important to note that Scripture regards government as one of God's good gifts to humankind. Government, says Paul in Romans 13, is "instituted" by God. The biblical writers never shy away from acknowledging that specific governments are often a great evil. Pharaoh oppressed the Israelites; the "beast" of Revelation

23

13 is a government that demands idolatrous obeisance from every-one, etc. But government, when it does what it is supposed to do, is a great good. Governmental authorities, says Paul in Romans 13, "are God's servants for your good." As such, they are to be "respected" and "honored."

It's important for those of us who live in the United States to let this last point sink in. There is, at present, a great deal of bad-mouthing by US citizens of their government. Government is seen as the enemy. And rather than government officials being respected and honored, they are demeaned, insulted, bullied. It's one thing to disagree; it's quite another thing to demean. All too often, Christians join the crowd in this bad-mouthing and demeaning. Apparently they have never read Romans 13—or if they have, it didn't sink in.

Back to our topic: what is government supposed to do? The theme that runs throughout Christian Scripture, Old Testament and New Testament alike, is that the main task of government is to secure jus-tice. (In a subsequent letter I will explain how I understand justice.) Nowhere do the biblical writers say that government must confine itself to securing justice; there is nothing wrong, for example, with government developing infrastructure that benefits society as a whole. But the central and indispensable task of government is to secure justice. Consider, for example, the picture of the good king in the opening verses of Psalm 72:

> Give the king your justice, O God,
> and your right-doing to a king's son.
> May he judge your people rightly,
> and your poor with justice....
> May he defend the cause of the poor of the people,
> give deliverance to the needy and crush the oppressor.

This understanding of the good ruler, as responsible for securing justice in society, is carried over into the New Testament when, for example, Paul says, in Romans 13, that government is the servant of God "to execute wrath on the wrongdoer." I think we would interpret Paul in much too pinched a fashion if we thought he meant to say that the sole task of government is punishment of wrongdoers. Just punishment takes place within a system of just laws justly administered. To establish and maintain such a system is the God-given task of government.

Thinking back to my first trip to Honduras, I recall going with you and some others from ASJ to the office of the Attorney General. What immediately struck me was that—wow!—ASJ was not just denouncing the government and pointing accusing fingers at corrupt officials. It was trying to get the Honduran government to do what government should be doing—and to assist it in doing that. What also struck me was the cordial relations between ASJ and the people in the Attorney General's office.

Explain to me those cordial relations. I did not expect that. As I mentioned in my first letter, working for social justice typically evokes hostility. Given those cordial relations, I would guess that there are some people following the work of ASJ who suspect that you are being co-opted.

Your friend,
Nick

6

Working with the Honduran Attorney General

Dear Nick,

Your question about how people respond to our work is a good one. And it's interesting that you mention our relation to the Honduran Attorney General, because the cordiality that you witnessed between us was hard-won. It's an interesting story as to how it came about, and one that I think is emblematic of the way ASJ works with, and not just in spite of, government systems.

Our relationship with the office of the Attorney General began in 2013, when ASJ co-director Carlos Hernández was invited to sit on a selection committee for Honduras' next Attorney General. Carlos had been outspoken in advocating for improved security and judicial systems, and his message was popular; his presence on the selection committee may have been an effort to win over people skeptical of the often politicized process. But Carlos was determined not to be anyone's pawn.

To select Honduras' Attorney General, different groups representing different sectors of Honduran society are allowed to nominate candidates, resulting in a broad pool of up to a hundred applicants. A seven-member selection committee, also made up of diverse sectors of society, narrows the list down to five finalists, and then sends the list to the National Congress for its members to make the final vote.

In the past, this multi-step process had been little more than a façade to pass the top candidates of the political elite on to Congress, where they would vote along party lines. But Carlos said that if he were to sit on this committee, it would have to be different.

One of the first things Carlos insisted on was that the committee evaluate candidates with the full battery of what in Honduras are called "confidence tests," which include a background check, drug test, psychometric evaluation, and polygraph test. These had never been administered to a candidate for such a high-ranking position, so we were all thrilled when the selection committee agreed to the tests.

On the committee, Carlos found common ground with Julieta Castellanos, director of the National University, and Ramón Custodio, the country's human rights ombudsman. The three of them voted "in block" to keep the committee on track, making transparent decisions and avoiding political intervention.

Everything was going remarkably well until they had winnowed the candidates down to about twenty. One of the members of the selection committee wasn't happy about the elimination of one of the applicants. He came to the next meeting demanding that Oscar Chinchilla, a political favorite closely aligned with the ruling party, be put back on the list.

Carlos, of course, refused. Carlos and his allies were happy with the way the process had been going. Chinchilla had been eliminated in accord with the process that the entire committee had agreed to. But when the issue came to a vote, Carlos, the university director, and the ombudsman's objections were outnumbered and the committee voted four to three to reincorporate him.

Now Carlos and his allies faced a difficult situation. Would they continue to participate in a process that they believed had been co-opted? Or would they face the personal and political consequences of taking a stand? They chose the latter, walking off the commission and immediately to a press conference, where they denounced the politicization of the process.

The next day, their resignation was the top story all over the news, bringing increased scrutiny to the selection process. But, in spite of the attention, the process continued, and the now-four-member selection committee sent their five candidates to Congress—with Chinchilla, who should have been eliminated, on that list.

The process in Congress was opaque and drawn out, with rumors of backroom deals and of money changing hands. Congress took a vote on Friday morning, but didn't announce its choice until the pre-dawn hours on Sunday. Squeaking through with just enough votes, Oscar Chinchilla became the new Attorney General.

Now if that was as far as our work with the government had gone, just denouncing corruption, this would have been a failure. All the attention and controversy we generated weren't enough to change the outcome. But our work *didn't* end there. We at ASJ feel responsible not just to call out corruption but to actively work to address it. So we asked for a meeting with Chinchilla. We laid out our priorities and suggestions for making the office of the Attorney General stronger.

It was an awkward meeting, but I think our motivations were clear. This wasn't a political game for us; we really cared about making the Attorney General's office effective, regardless of who was Attorney General. I think Chinchilla respected that.

Here's where the story gets really interesting: it turned out that, in spite of the irregularities of his election, Chinchilla wasn't going to "play nice" with government authorities. Just weeks after his swearing in, the Attorney General's office seized half a billion dollars in assets owned by the notorious drug trafficking group known as "the Cachiros." This was huge—it was the first time Honduras had seized assets funded by drug trafficking, and it was the first of many asset seizures his office would carry out.

Surprising us, and, I think, surprising many politicians, Chinchilla has become one of the strongest Attorney Generals in Central America, particularly in the crucial areas of drug trafficking and gang violence. His office is touching people in the same powerful political groups that had brought him to power. Under his management, the Attorney General's office signed an extradition treaty with the United States, and has extradited more than forty Honduran drug traffickers, including the son of a former president. The office has broken up previously untouchable cartels, and has seized millions of dollars' worth of goods bought with illicit funds—more than the Honduran government had ever recovered before.

Chinchilla knows we have a close eye on him; but he also knows we are willing to support him on initiatives that are just and transparent. We collaborated on a public campaign called "No to Corruption" that sought to raise awareness about how citizens could report the corruption that they observed. We frequently hold training sessions to build up the capacities of public prosecutors and investigators. We offer constant legal support and expertise.

This relationship hasn't always been smooth. At times, we are frustrated by insufficient access to information. At times, Chinchilla feels our criticisms against his office are too strong. There continues to be a healthy professional distance between our two organizations; but throughout this back and forth, give and take, we have been consistent: if Chinchilla is really committed to justice, we will have his back.

This became incredibly important as Chinchilla continued to take on high profile cases, including the arrest of twenty-two Honduran mayors. As he leads this work, he walks a near-impossible political tightrope between gangs and organized criminals, and the politicians linked closely with them. By being more independent and active than anyone had expected, Chinchilla has almost no one in his corner, which makes ASJ's support all the more crucial.

When Chinchilla and his family received death threats, he confided in Carlos, who had received similar threats. Carlos encouraged him and prayed with him. When his mother lay dying in the hospital, Carlos came and sat with him for hours—in that moment, no one talked about politics.

When I think about our relationship with the Attorney General, I think about theologian John Calvin's assertion that, like Jesus, all of us are prophets, priests, and kings, exerting different forms of authority in different situations. I also realize that God often uses us in ways very different from what we might have envisioned!

When Carlos took his place on that selection committee, that was a political action—a manifestation of the kingly authority Calvin talks about. When Carlos walked off the selection committee, he was fulfilling a prophetic authority not to entertain corruption in any form. When Carlos sat by the hospital bed of the Attorney General's mother, his message was very different—it was a priestly authority in which he laid aside political differences and ministered to the Attorney General as a brother.

I think the intersection among these three roles is what has led ASJ to the achievements we've seen in this country—but it's a constant balancing act. When does ASJ need to be a prophetic voice and denounce injustice? When does ASJ need to be a priestly voice and sit down at the table for dialogue? When does it need to be a kingly voice and cooperate from within government structures?

Much of the public wants us to throw stones and spend all our time calling out injustices. Many groups spend all their time doing just that. But when I think about the pressures the Attorney General faced, and continues to face, in his position, I'm convinced that a constant barrage of stones is not what will lead to change.

We want government systems to work. I think we have to recognize that these systems are made up of human beings who, like any of us, need a place to turn to, and moments where they, too, can be listened to and supported.

Recently Oscar Chinchilla gave a press conference about his office's results over the past few years. "I want to thank various groups who have accompanied us ..." he said, "in particular, the Asociación para una Sociedad más Justa, which I believe has taught us a lesson—sometimes you need to point out things that are bad; but at other times you should work hand in hand to make changes and advocate for improvement."

Hearing that from him, a neat summation of our own philosophy of change, reinforced in me a sense of the importance of our threefold role. As kings, priests, and prophets, we can bring about change.

I hope that answers your question about our relationship with government. You were surprised that there was not more hostility. I hope I have shown both the value of cooperating with government and the reality that the process of reaching a cordial relationship is certainly not easy. As someone who has worn more a practitioner's hat than an academic one throughout my career, I see the role of government in a practical way—as an institution charged with protecting the rights and well-being of its citizens.

Your friend,
Kurt

7

ASJ Stands Up For, and Stands Alongside, the Marginalized

Dear Kurt

Not only did I find your story about the emerging relation of Carlos Hernandez to the Attorney General very moving in its own right; I also found very illuminating your identification of three distinct roles that Carlos has played. I must admit that it had never occurred to me to distinguish those three distinct ways of getting government to do what it ought to do. I think you are right, that the interweaving of those three ways of relating to the government is distinctive of ASJ's work and a considerable clue to its success.

As you note, it takes great wisdom to know when to exercise which of these three roles. What impresses me about the work of ASJ is not only that it quite self-consciously plays all three of these roles, but that it has been extraordinarily sure-footed in deciding when to play which role. I dare say you can point to mistakes that have been made along the way. But those mistakes have obviously not impeded the overall success of ASJ.

I also very much liked your bringing Calvin's discussion of the threefold office of the believer into the discussion: prophet, priest, and king. That gives theological "heft" to the threefold relation of ASJ to the government. (Calvin was, of course, using the terms metaphorically. His discussion is to be found in Book II, chapter xv, of his *Institutes of the Christian Religion*).

There is one aspect of the work of ASJ that I think should be highlighted more than it has been up to this point in our conversation. You do mention it; but I think it merits additional emphasis.

It would be possible to act in the threefold way you identify when defending big corporations against each other or against the government. That is most definitely not what ASJ does. It consistently has its eye on what the laws and practices of Honduras do to what you call the "marginalized," the "vulnerable," the "oppressed"—what the writers of the Old Testament typically call the "downtrodden." In trying to get the government to do what it ought to do, ASJ consistently stands up for the downtrodden and their rights.

But that does not capture the whole of what ASJ has done over the years. There is another aspect of its work that does not fit comfortably within the threefold relation of ASJ to the government. Sometimes ASJ has not only *stood up for* the marginalized in its work with the government. Sometimes it has *stood alongside* particular members of the marginalized.

I have in mind, for example, the work you described in your first letter, of securing land titles for those living in a particular section of Tegucigalpa. ASJ discovered that the way in which poor property owners were being victimized was not a piecemeal problem but a systemic problem. Accordingly, it helped to draft and pass legislation that changed the way in which all land disputes in Honduras are settled. But it did more than that: it stood alongside individual property owners, assisting them in negotiating the legal maze to get official deeds to their property. I shall never forget being guided through that section of Tegucigalpa by a team from ASJ, and seeing residents standing in their doorways proudly displaying their deeds. I also remember, from that first visit, hearing of the refusal of poor people in Honduras, out of fear of retaliation, to come forward as witnesses to crimes, and of the ingenious ways that ASJ was coping with that fear in individual cases.

A full description of the work of ASJ would be that it not only tries to get government to do what government is supposed to do, namely, secure justice, but it also sometimes stands alongside particular victims of injustice to obtain their rights.

The theoretical questions posed at this point are, obviously, what is justice, what are rights, and how are justice and rights related to each other? I want to address those questions. But before I do, I would like to hear more from you, Kurt, about how ASJ works. In particular, I would like some more examples of how ASJ both critiques and supports government. The way in which Carlos related to the Attorney General is one example. But I would like to get a more general picture of how ASJ operates.

Your friend,
Nick

8

How ASJ Critiques and Supports Government in Doing Its Work

Dear Nick,

You asked for concrete examples of how ASJ has prodded and assisted government officials to fulfill their responsibilities. As I thought about this, I found that our interactions and interventions with the Honduran government generally fell into four different categories, with varying degrees of cooperation from government officials: uninvited critiques, audits by invitation, accompaniment and technical assistance, and finally, substitution of government functions, which we have taken on only in emergency and short-term transitional cases.

Which of these four interventions we use depends both on the government's capacity and their openness to our investigations and critiques. As I share a few examples, I'm sure you will see that each method of intervention carries its advantages and disadvantages, and that we have to constantly discern which is appropriate for each instance of corruption or government weakness.

Critiques of Government

Direct, public critiques of government actions or policies are perhaps the most common intervention in the advocacy world and require no openness from the government itself. In many ways, this intervention is the most instinctual. When we observe an injustice, we want to bring it to light, and we hope that public attention and outcry will bring about change.

When ASJ began its work in education, we carried out an investigation that discovered that many schools were meeting for just 125 days in class per year instead of the 200 days mandated by law. In addition, 26 percent of teachers on payroll could not be found in classrooms. After we reviewed the data, we took it public. We held a press conference, and dozens of journalists attended—the story made national news and generated public outrage. The government tried to ignore us at first. It took months of pressure before the President eventually took action and replaced the Minister of Education. The new Minister, Marlon Escoto, perhaps wanting to avoid a similar scandal, was then very open to our suggestions for reforms.

Our criticism of the Ministry of Health faced even more severe opposition. While the Ministry of Education was initially unresponsive, the Ministry of Health was openly hostile. Our priority in health was uncovering why medicines purchased by the Honduran government were not finding their way to Honduran hospitals. When we released our findings at a public conference, public officials in attendance shouted that we were liars, and threw chairs in anger.

We pressed on undeterred, looking into the process of selecting, processing, storing, and distributing medicines. We took cases of corruption to the minister at the time, Arturo Bendaña. He was belligerent, even threatening. However, we knew that what we had uncovered was affecting millions of people's access to medicine. So, in spite of his lack of openness, we pressed forward with a public presentation. Again, the media picked up our story, and again, it made big waves.

Bendaña ultimately resigned from his post, and the President tried three replacements, none of whom had the will or ability to make the foundational changes that the Ministry of Health needed. However, our advocacy did put us in a position to help implement important reforms in the way that medicines are purchased and distributed.

Of course, not every public critique leads so neatly to acquiescence from political leaders. For years, we have denounced mistreatment of security guards. One of our lawyers, Dionisio Díaz García, was killed for pursuing this work. Despite more than a decade of advocacy, however, the government has failed to make substantial reforms in the investigation of labor rights abuses. Nonetheless, we continue in this advocacy, not because there is openness from the government, or because we see potential for immediate change, but because it is just. In any government, there will always be a space for this type of intervention.

Audits of Government

In our early days as an organization, nearly all of our actions were public critiques like those mentioned above. However, as we continued to take cases public, our credibility increased to the point where government institutions responded more favorably to our critiques—and even sought out our advice directly, sometimes even before we held a press conference. Our shift to auditing, and not just denouncing, government systems was not simply opportunistic; as we matured as an organization, we also learned that it was often much more effective to first address problems through private conversations than through generating public scandals.

The institutions' motivations for seeking out our help were not purely selfless; government officials face constant pressure to protect their reputation and seek re-election, and an apparent openness to transparency reflects well on them. But we also found that some government leaders genuinely felt overwhelmed by corruption in their ministries and welcomed help with identifying concrete steps for improvement. They were in need of fresh ideas, and they wanted the legitimacy of an outside group to take some of the pressure off their ordering and later implementing those changes.

This is best evidenced by a groundbreaking agreement signed in 2014 with ASJ, Transparency International, and the Honduran government, which authorized ASJ to carry out audits of five major government institutions, evaluating them by their compliance with legal and administrative standards for things like major purchases, human resources, and the management of public information.

Our detailed analyses, crafted after reviewing tens of thousands of pages of documentation and hundreds of hours of interviews, have uncovered irregularities, inefficiencies, and occasionally, blatant instances of corruption. Our investigations have uncovered "ghost" employees who never show up to work, needlessly specific calls for bids that prevent competition for million-dollar government purchases, and vehicles purchased with public money that end up in the garages of public officials—all instances of corruption that together can drain millions of dollars from Honduras' most essential government services.

We presented all these findings publicly; however, the key difference from "critiquing" government is that the findings were accompanied not just by our recommendations but by a complementary improvement plan designed in partnership with the institution's leaders. The results weren't a surprise to the ministers—we had gone to them first with our findings and our recommendations. This didn't change the result of our advocacy, but it did allow them a head start to present a public improvement plan.

Our intention for government audits is not to disgrace or shame the ministers who have cooperated with us to collect often damaging information. We highlight not just instances of corruption, but also strengths of the institutions, and give ministers the opportunity to commit publicly to a detailed plan for improvement. This opportunity to save face and commit to improvement is the carrot to the stick of our critical denunciations before the Honduran public. Many public officials have responded to this strategy. Seeing that we are not openly hostile toward them, many more are open to work with us to implement incremental improvements in their institutions.

After our baseline report, and a joint plan for improvement, we returned eighteen months later to carry out a second baseline evaluation. In every institution, we have found significant advances. The payroll for the entire security sector used to be managed from a single Excel spreadsheet on a laptop with no password protection. Now, the security sector uses a top human resources management software. Hiring of education administrators used to be a politicized and corrupt process. New reforms hold hiring processes to predefined, merit-based standards. The Ministry of Health has completely overhauled the way it purchases and distributes medicines, reducing theft and loss. Overall, we've seen the performance scores of our target institutions rise by an average of 26 percent in just three years.

We find government audits with follow-up plans to be extremely useful for strengthening institutions, rooting out corruption, and, ultimately, offering more and better services to the poor. Regardless, this intervention isn't easy. Some people are morally opposed to co-operating with an institution where corruption is rampant. Others dismiss us as naïve for thinking we can make a difference, or accuse us of legitimizing a corrupt government. This is a constant tension, especially as we move from audits and recommendations to more direct accompaniment.

Accompanying Government

In our work with the government, we have found that the lack of a will to improve is often not the only barrier to structural improvement. Some government agencies avoid change because the benefits from a corrupt status quo outweigh the costs of changing. But others would be willing to change if they had the resources, training, or technical expertise to do so. Our commitment to address these latter challenges is something that sets ASJ apart from most advocacy and anti-corruption organizations. Many NGOs will critique the government, but few are actively working to implement needed changes.

In the Ministry of Education, for example, critiques of too few days in class, absentee teachers, and other issues led to a public outcry and the minister stepping down. Escoto, the new minister, was open to our suggestions but lacked the ability to implement them. When he came to office, one of the first things he did was ask for our help.

It would have been easier and less messy for us to leave the situation as we had denounced it. We had done our work of bringing the corruption to light—the Honduran public was aware of the situation and demanded a solution. However, our ultimate goal has always been to see government systems work. So when Escoto asked for our help, we agreed to go a step further and walk alongside the Minister's personnel as they implemented reforms. Our experts in human resources supported an audit of all personnel, purging teacher payrolls of absentee teachers. Our experts in government contracting found weaknesses in the ways that textbooks and school supplies were purchased and delivered to schools, resulting in better use of the public budget. In 2013, schools across Honduras met and passed the 200-day benchmark and the resulting increase in class time has translated to better educational outcomes for Honduran children.

This is just one example of how we currently accompany the Honduran government in its implementation of more transparent and efficient management structures. We have found that our willingness to volunteer time and energy to walk alongside government officials as they implement these changes can be the difference between a reformed institution and a simply discredited one.

Doing the Government's Work

The final category is actually carrying out work that pertains to the government. Our mission as an organization is to help make government systems work, not to create parallel systems, so this is always an intervention of last resort. There has to be agreement among government authorities, our organization, and the general population, that there is a drastic breakdown in the public system and that outside intervention is necessary. In addition, this intervention must always be temporary, with a clear plan to strengthening the public system to the point where it can recover its functions.

One example of this type of intervention is in the reform of the National Police. The police force in Honduras was long seen as a lost cause—different administrations had made attempts to "purge" the police of corruption, generally spending millions of dollars to fire just a few low-ranking cops. In 2016, however, when evidence emerged that the top brass were involved in a murder-for-hire scheme, everyone agreed that *something* had to be done. However, they also agreed that a police force so corrupt couldn't be trusted to reform itself. So the President asked us. Two of our staff members and two of our board members were invited to serve on a Special Commission charged with reforming and restructuring the entire police force.

The civilian-led Special Commission has removed thousands of compromised officers, restructured broken systems, and passed better policing laws. But the Commission is temporary by nature. Now, after two years, the Commission's goal is to build up leadership in the police and the Ministry of Security so that they can oversee ongoing improvements.

We do not take these intervening roles lightly. While the potential benefits are high—imagine being given free rein to implement reforms you've long called for—the risks are also very high. Such a position is physically dangerous, as we speak out against powerful people with connections to drug traffickers and organized crime. It is also politically dangerous, as we walk the line between cooperating closely with a government administration while also remaining independent and critical of it. Looking back now, our entry into the reform process seems natural; however, we had to have many serious conversations before agreeing. "Are we being set up to fail?" we asked ourselves. We knew we could hurt our organization and everything we had worked to build. We were also wary of being used as political pawns—giving legitimacy to a process that was less than transparent.

At ASJ, we have always tried to avoid short-term Band-Aid solutions. We want to see reforms in the underlying legal structure, reforms in structures of management and administration, in manuals and guidebooks, and in the culture and transparency of institutions. While we would be thrilled to see the Honduran government make these changes on their own, or at our recommendation, ultimately we are open to direct participation if and when we can be assured that these fundamental reforms will take place.

There's a hopefulness to this attitude. Even when we see government systems so broken down that they seem incapable of fixing their own problems, we respond not with wanting to burn the government to the ground, but by temporarily taking the mantle on our own shoulders in order to build it back up. It's a position we take on rarely—always after much prayer and discernment, always in cooperation with other members of civil society, and always on a temporary basis, with the goal of shifting responsibility back to the government where it belongs.

Choosing the Right Method

As ASJ moves between these different categories of intervention, we have learned that a rising level of influence frequently coincides with a rising level of criticism. Most Hondurans are pleased when we critique government; many believe that we should audit government; but fewer are comfortable with accompanying the government in reforms, or with taking on reform activities ourselves. Too often it appears to them that we are taking the side of a specific political party. We know we are always doing our best to strengthen the state and its institutions, not a political party; but this explanation can often fall on deaf ears.

As we have done this work, we have become increasingly convinced of the necessity of credible, qualified, nonpartisan citizens working alongside weak governments. We have seen time and time again that civil servants, regardless of their intentions, must operate within institutional cultures and structures that don't always allow for innovation or reform. Often, it is outsiders who must push for the reforms that political and economic elites operating within corrupt structures and institutions would never allow on their own.

Our staff are experts in their fields, but more than that, they are motivated not by politics, spite, or personal ambition—but by their faith in a just God, and by a desire to see systems work and the country they love become a better place.

I have described a method of working that includes supporting the government, and even, temporarily, stepping in to do its work. In a culture where any closeness to the government can be construed as condoning that government, this has certainly won us criticism. This makes me wonder, Nick, how you see this tension relating to the difference between retributive and restorative justice. We see our work as primarily about restoration—improving results, increasing effectiveness, and building up trust in government institutions.

This seems like the longest-reaching and most kingdom-centric goal. However, especially in an environment of oppression and injustice, the desire for retribution is strong, and it's difficult not to rejoice when a particularly egregious offender faces prison or extradition. How does one manage this tension in justice work—the tension between restoring systems and holding the corrupt accountable for the damage they have done in breaking them?

Your friend,
Kurt

9

Affinity between the Goals of ASJ and Those of the Restorative Justice Movement

Dear Kurt,

That was a superb summary of how ASJ works. Thank you for it. I came away with a very clear understanding of what one might call "The ASJ model."

In the last paragraph of your letter you observe that while the work of ASJ is primarily aimed at the restoration of institutions in situations of injustice, the desire for retribution and not just restoration is often strong in such situations. And that leads you to pose two questions to me. How can an institution such as ASJ manage the tension between restoring systems and holding the corrupt accountable? And how do I see that tension related to the difference between retributive justice and a rather recent development in the practice of justice that is now commonly called *restorative* justice? Presumably you ask this latter question because you sense that ASJ's goals of restoration are in harmony with the practices of restorative justice, but in tension with retributive justice.

The difference between retributive and restorative justice is an important and complex topic in its own right. So let me, in this letter, describe these two forms of justice and the difference between them; and then, in my next letter, let me speak to the tension you experience in the work of ASJ and the relation of that tension to the difference between retributive and restorative justice.

Retributive justice and restorative justice are two distinct forms of what I call *second-order* justice. Already in Greek antiquity, writers distinguished between two fundamentally different forms of

43

justice. One consists of justice in our ordinary relations with each other—teachers and students treating each other justly, merchants and clients treating each other justly, etc. Call this *first-order* justice. The other form of justice becomes relevant when there has been a violation of first-order justice. Call that *second-order* justice. (In some of my writings I have called these "primary justice" and "secondary justice.")

Second-order justice commonly takes the form of punishment, with punishment, in general, being the imposition of hard treatment on someone for their having treated someone unjustly—for their having wronged someone. In different societies and in different times, the hard treatment has taken many different forms: whipping, public mockery, exile, shunning, banning, torture, imprisonment, execution, and more besides.

Why is punishment of a wrongdoer thought to be an appropriate response to his or her act of wrongdoing? What's the point, the rationale, of imposing hard treatment on someone for their act of wronging someone?

Traditionally, the most common rationale, by far, has been the *retribution* rationale. Our word *retribution* comes from the Latin *retribuere*, meaning "to pay back." The idea is that when a wrongdoer is justly punished, the wrongdoer is paid back for the injury he imposed on his victim with an equivalent hard treatment imposed on the wrongdoer.

And why repay harm with harm, injury with injury? What's the point? Most people nowadays who think in terms of retribution would probably be at a loss to answer this question. Writers in the ancient world had an explanation. They thought that wrongdoing created an imbalance in the moral order that had to be corrected by the imposition of a harm on the wrongdoer equivalent to the harm he imposed on his victim. Understood in this way, punishment is an *intrinsically* moral activity, not an activity whose morality depends on its effects on society or the wrongdoer. And it was thought to be *morally required* as a response to an act of wrongdoing. The imbalance in the moral order created by wrongdoing *must be* corrected.

Of course punishment can be—and often is—a violation of how a person should be treated. But punishment of the right sort, so it has commonly been assumed, is an intrinsically moral act that is morally required as a response to an act of wrongdoing. "He's getting what he *deserves*."

In the modern world, a number of thinkers and writers have rejected retribution as the rationale for punishment, typically because the idea of repaying harm with harm seems to them archaic, regressive, incompatible with progressive ways of thinking. But rather than identifying something else about punishment that makes it an intrinsically moral activity, they have instead fastened on the beneficial consequences that punishment can bring about.

One such consequentialist rationale for punishment is the *reform* rationale: the point of imposing hard treatment on a wrongdoer is to reform him or her. That was the rationale behind the establishment of so-called *penitentiaries* and *reformatories* in the US in the nineteenth century.

Another consequentialist rationale is the *deterrence* rationale: the point of imposing hard treatment on a wrongdoer is to deter others from doing what he did.

A third consequentialist rationale is the *protection* rationale: society has to be protected from the wrongdoer engaging in additional acts of wrongdoing.

Now consider all four of these rationales together: retribution, reform, deterrence, and protection. And then notice that the fundamental point of each of them is to uphold, each in its own way, the order of moral or civil law. The order of law is upheld by restoring balance to the moral order, by reforming the wrongdoer so that he will no longer violate the law, by deterring others from similar violations of the law, and/or by protecting society from additional violations of the law by the wrongdoer. Wrongdoing is thought to be not only a *violation* of the order of law but a *threat* to the order of law. The point of punishment is to protect the order of law against that threat.

I can now bring restorative justice into the picture. Notice that, in the above four rationales for punishment, no mention was made of the victim, only of the wrongdoer and of the law he or she violated. But when someone commits an act of wrongdoing, they not only violate some law but also *wrong someone, wrong a person.* Or more ac-curately: almost always they wrong a number of people, not just the victim but also family, friends, neighbors, and so forth. They create a breach in personal relationships. (An exception: there are so-called *victimless crimes,* like breaking the speed limit.)

Punishment, whatever its rationale, pays no attention to that breach in personal relationships. Restorative justice, by contrast, focuses on healing the breach in personal relationships wreaked by wrongdoing. It does not oppose all punishment. But its focus is not on punishing the wrongdoer for his violation of the law but on heal-ing the breach in personal relationships that his wrongdoing created.

How can that breach be healed? By the wrongdoer acknowledg-ing the wrong he has done, taking responsibility for it, repenting of it, expressing his repentance in the form of apologizing, by making amends when that is relevant—and by the victim and the others who have been wronged by him accepting his apology and forgiving him for what he did to them. When this interpersonal transaction takes place, the breach is healed. The parties are reconciled.

That makes it sound easy: the wrongdoer apologizes and makes amends, the victim and the others who have been wronged forgive, and the parties are reconciled. But often it's not easy. The wrongdoer resists taking responsibility for the wrong he did and resists apolo-gizing: he couldn't help it, he says, or it wasn't his fault, or the victim had it coming. Or some or all of those who have been wronged resist forgiving: "May he rot in hell for what he did!" So this is where the work of those who practice restorative justice comes into the pic-ture: the work of trying to bring the resistant wrongdoer to the point where he takes responsibility for the wrong he did and apologizes and makes amends, or the work of trying to bring the resistant victim and the others who have been wronged to the point where they are able and willing to forgive. Often it's hard work, often it takes a long time, often it's only partly successful. And in the case of homicide, the wrongdoer may seek reconciliation with the family and friends of the victim, but with the victim herself there cannot be reconciliation.

To anticipate a point that I will be making in my next letter: there is, indeed, the tension that you sense, Kurt, between the restorative work of ASJ and the exercise of retributive justice, which repays harm with harm. But between ASJ's restorative work and the practice of restorative justice there is deep affinity. They fit together hand in glove.

And now I have a question for you that I've been wanting to ask for some time. An important component of ASJ's overall strategy has been bringing public pressure to bear on officials who are falling down on their jobs. Corrupt and ineffective officials seldom respond to sweet reasoning. There has to be pressure. I would like to hear more about how you have stirred up and mobilized public pressure. From your description thus far, it all sounds quite genteel. Several times you have mentioned press conferences. Have there also been marches, rallies, demonstrations, and the like, designed to stir up anger in the public and bring pressure to bear on public officials? The public does have to get angry, does it not, in order for serious change to occur?

Your friend,
Nick

IO

Mobilizing Public Pressure

Dear Nick,

Thanks for your questions. While in my previous letter I gave you a general picture of how ASJ works, it's worth going into more detail about using pressure on public officials in order to promote change.

ASJ has held some marches and rallies that express public outrage, but this has not usually been our principal focus. Those sorts of public events are risky. It's difficult to anticipate how many people will participate. It's difficult to control the message, or keep it from being hijacked or misinterpreted. ASJ's philosophy has always been to connect broken systems to concrete and actionable proposals. Those proposals can seldom be summed up in chants and slogans.

That is not to say that these popular movements don't exist in Honduras. Notably, in 2015, a group of people called the *Indignados* or "the Indignant" led marches of over 100,000 people, taking to the streets to protest the theft of hundreds of millions of dollars from the country's social security fund. The movement successfully brought the scandal to international attention, but though the protests lasted for months and successfully brought international attention, eventually they disbanded. The government made some concessions, for example, allowing the formation of the "MACCIH," an international corruption commission, but most of the demands around the scandal were all but swept under the rug.

We've seen this in movements such as Occupy Wall Street. The same factors that give these social movements broad appeal—general complaints, lack of clear demands, lack of hierarchies or clear leadership—also limit their effectiveness in accomplishing real structural reforms.

When ASJ taps into or mobilizes public anger, it is much more commonly through bringing information and statistics to the national media, and thus into the minds and opinions of the general public. As we bring our discoveries and research to newspapers, radio, and television channels, we see our findings begin to shape the dialogue around the reforms we hope to see.

Regarding the Honduran education system, for example, there was never any shortage of anger or frustration by the public. Only about 40 percent of Honduran students perform at their grade level in math and reading, and everyone from parents to teachers to international organizations complained about the government's inability to educate Honduran youth. But these complaints were abstract. They were not specifically directed to anyone, except perhaps "the government" in general.

It's true that politicians held responsibility for Honduras' failing education system. But in a 2013 study, ASJ identified another culprit—the teacher's unions, which had evolved from institutions meant to ensure teachers' rights to bully institutions that mandated membership and called for strikes as many as seventy-five days per year. ASJ's study also found that 26 percent of teachers on the government payroll couldn't be found in the classroom at all. Some of the missing teachers sub-contracted others to teach their classes for them—others collected salaries and failed to show up at all.

Carefully combing through education laws and regulations, ASJ found that Honduran schools were required to provide children with 200 days of class per year. No one in the general public talked about this, and few knew that the law existed. But the disparity between the 125 days of class children were receiving and the 200 days of class required was so striking that we centered our messaging on it.

We started with a press conference, where we presented three bombshell studies that provided evidence about who should be held responsible for missed days of school, absent teachers, and poor control in hiring and management practices. It was not, in your words, genteel. In fact, the reason why we published all three studies at once was that one of our allies advised us that after publishing even one of them, we could expect angry unions to spray-paint our offices, break our windows, and threaten us to the point where we wouldn't want to publish any more.

We released a huge quantity of information, detailed and specific, naming individual schools, teachers, and offenses. We also shaped our messaging in a way that we knew would be accessible and compelling to the population. We coined the term "ghost teachers" to describe teachers who received a salary without showing up to class, and demanded "200 days of class," turning an unknown requirement into a national rallying cry.

We were invited to top TV news programs, interviewed by newspapers and radio programs. We were willing to name names, we had evidence of the problems, we could cite statistics, and we weren't afraid of making specific demands. This information was received by Hondurans across the country, and the clamor was such that government officials were forced to respond. The minister was forced to step down, and the new one worked closely with ASJ in carrying out one of the first comprehensive censuses of Honduran teachers. In a single year, he eliminated 26,000 nonworking teachers from the outdated payroll of 82,000, and ensured that, for the first time, all schools met for 200 days.

Another example of one of our more public campaigns was our intervention in the public health sector. Knowing that despite spending millions, public hospitals almost never had medicines that patients needed, we began to research exactly why. After months of requesting information and analyzing reams of public contracts, we uncovered that medicines purchased by the Honduran government were wildly overpriced, and frequently accompanied by 30–40 percent "kickbacks" to the authorities in charge, inflating the cost of medicines even more. Furthermore, chemical analysis of the pills being purchased revealed medicines whose active ingredients were expired, too weak, or missing entirely.

Again, we took this information public. We were not expecting a genteel reception, and we certainly did not get one. A top official in the health sector actually threw a chair after hearing our accusations; the Minister of Health sent men in suits to intimidate us from continuing our investigation. This was serious; people who had previously asked questions about the health sector had been killed. We even heard from an employee of one of the pharmaceutical companies that one of the medicine companies had hired hit men to kill Carlos Hernández, my best friend and co-director at ASJ.

But we pressed ahead. We made television appearances and gave quotes to newspapers. Once again, we had a shocking story and we weren't afraid to tell it. We found ways to distill a complex issue into a few key talking points that average late-night television viewers could understand and organize behind. One of the reasons Carlos Hernández received such serious threats was that, on a national television program, he took a blood pressure pill and crumbled it in his fingers, showing how the life-saving medicine was made with white powder. Now, years later, when people talk about corruption in the health sector, they still refer to those "flour pills."

Once again, the public responded with outrage. And soon the tenor of our conversation with authorities began to change. The Minister who had sent his henchmen to threaten us now called Carlos and me in tears, begging us think of the reputation of his family. He was let go soon after, and two more ministers were hired and fired in quick succession, a sign both that the government felt the need to be seen doing something and that they had little clear idea of what to do.

Our pressure eventually brought about some of the results we were looking for. Police arrested the director of the medicines warehouse, a woman who for twenty-two years had abused her position to enrich herself through theft and corruption. Charges were brought against the family of the vice president of Congress, whose medicine company ASJ had shown to be involved in the sale of exorbitantly priced, low-quality medicines. Finally, under pressure, the government invited the United Nations to oversee purchasing of all medicines for public hospitals in a special trust set up with one of the country's most prestigious banks and overseen by ASJ auditors. These changes not only held powerful people accountable, but they saved the state approximately $90 million by ensuring that they were purchasing medicines at fair market prices.

This sort of work is emblematic of ASJ interventions, and it is rarely, to use your word, genteel. Government officials are always upset to be publicly linked to crime and corruption. They risk losing public support, political power, or even—less commonly, but importantly—may face criminal charges. Resistance by entities outside of the government, unions or private companies, is often even more dangerous. Government employees are accustomed to public scrutiny to a certain extent. Private companies are not—and I think it's telling that some of the most risk we have faced as an organization has been due to backlash from business leaders.

When I think of how ASJ has influenced the general public around these big issues, I don't think back to any particular rally or public event. Instead, I think of how one single statistic—that only 4 percent of homicides were being solved—has become central to the national debate around violence and justice. I think of people in rural communities who begin demanding that their child get their full 200 days of class. Our research influences public perception and shifts the needle on public pressure, even when people do not recognize our organization's name. In the end, truth has power. We have found that good, well-evidenced, relevant statistics have a viral nature that helps put pressure on political leaders far beyond what we would be able to do alone.

This strategy of careful investigation coupled with public denunciation may have to be tweaked somewhat to work in Chicago or Nairobi. Maybe it would have to be tweaked in a "post-truth" world where even "irrefutable" facts and statistics are called into question. But I do believe that this overall strategy is one way to step closer to justice, wherever you are in the world.

Your friend,
Kurt

PART 2

JUSTICE, LOVE, AND FORGIVENESS

Rejecting Retribution

Dear Kurt,

The examples of corruption that you describe are hard to hear. One can understand why people want the wrongdoers punished. And that brings me to the questions you put to me in your letter before this last one, namely "how does one manage the tension in justice work ... between restoring systems and holding the corrupt accountable," and how is that tension related to the difference between retributive and restorative justice?

In my discussion of restorative justice I noted that those who practice restorative justice are not opposed to punishment. Though, as we saw, their focus is not on punishment, they recognize that punishment is sometimes appropriate. The fact that there is a deep affinity between the restorationist goals of ASJ and the strategies of restorative justice does not imply that ASJ does not face the challenge you pose, namely, how to manage the tension between seeking restoration of systems and seeking the appropriate and just punishment of wrongdoers. Can a single organization do both of these? My answer is that yes it can, provided that punishment is not understood as retribution.

I retain a vivid memory of an episode that occurred in the course of my first visit to Tegucigalpa to observe the work of ASJ. One afternoon, we were driven up into the hills above the central city of Tegucigalpa to an area, Villa Nueva, where ASJ was focusing its criminal justice work, and invited into a neat, clean, and humble living room. The walls were cement block, the floor was packed earth—and, to my great delight, there were a number of brightly colored posters attached to the walls. Humble beauty!

The small room was crowded. Two women spoke of the rape of their daughters, and told of how the police refused to do anything until ASJ intervened; the perpetrators were eventually discovered, apprehended, and convicted. A young man spoke of being shot and wounded, and told of how, in his case too, the police refused to do anything until ASJ intervened; the perpetrators were discovered, apprehended, and convicted. There was great joy in the room, and not a dry eye.

You asked me afterwards whether it was right to take joy in the punishment of criminals. That led me to recall your mentioning to me, a few days earlier, that one of the criticisms ASJ was getting from some Christians in Honduras for its criminal justice work was that Christians should not be involved in the business of seeking the punishment of criminals. Rather than seeking punishment, they should forgive. If there is to be punishment, leave it to God. I took your word for this, but I was surprised. In the US, evangelical and conservative Christians have the reputation—rightly or wrongly—of being "tough on crime" and of supporting the policies that have led to our crisis of mass incarceration.

I was on the point of replying that it seemed to me thoroughly appropriate to rejoice at the apprehension and punishment of the criminals we had just heard about. ASJ had been working hard for the reform of the criminal justice system in Honduras. The stories we heard were stories about the proper workings of the system—albeit under considerable prodding by ASJ. We should rejoice that, in these cases, the system had eventually worked as it should.

I was, as I say, on the point of making that reply; but I didn't. It felt—well—superficial. Your question raised deep issues; it was not to be answered with a quick remark.

In my preceding letter I alluded to the fact that, in the Western way of thinking about punishment, one finds two persistent themes. First, retribution—repaying harm with harm—is an intrinsically moral activity. It may also have good consequences for the wrongdoer and for society. But whether or not it has those desirable consequences, retribution, so it has been thought, is an intrinsically moral activity. Second, unless the wrongdoing is trivial, punishment is morally required; it's not an option.

I noted that there are writers in the modern world who reject these principles. But there can be no doubt that they have been persistent themes in the way we in the West have thought about second-order justice, and that they continue to be embraced by many members of the public. "He's getting what he deserves." "He's got it coming."

I have come to the view that Christian Scripture rejects both of these principles. Insofar as Christians have accepted either one of them—and it is my impression that traditionally most Christians have—they have thought along pagan lines rather than listening carefully to the message of Scripture and drawing out its implications. In this letter, let me discuss the principle I mentioned first, namely, that retribution is an intrinsically moral activity.

Hovering in the background of Jesus' so-called Sermon on the Mount, as reported in Matthew and Luke, is what I have called, in my book *Justice in Love*, the "reciprocity code." The reciprocity code says that good is to be repaid with good and harm with harm. Evidently the code was prominent in the thought of those whom Jesus was addressing, as it was among the pagan Greeks and Romans.

Concerning the positive side of the code—return good with good—Jesus' response is a shrug of the shoulders. For the most part, returning good with good is a fine thing to do, especially among friends: repay a dinner party with a dinner party. But it's no big deal. Pretty much everybody accepts the principle: sinners, tax collectors, Gentiles, they all return good for good. "If you do good to those who do good to you, what credit is that to you? For even sinners do the same" (Luke 6:33). Don't be rigid about it, however. Don't let the principle prevent you from including in your dinner invitations those who cannot return the favor (Luke 14:12–14).

Jesus' attitude toward the negative side of the reciprocity code—the principle of retribution—was flat-out rejection. Returning evil for evil, repaying harm with harm, is out. One is always to do good; one is to love one's neighbor, even if the neighbor is an enemy who has treated one maliciously. "Love your enemies, do good to those who hate you" (Luke 6:27).

Jesus' rejection of retribution is echoed in the letters of the New Testament. In 1 Peter 3:9 we read, "Do not repay evil for evil or abuse for abuse; but, on the contrary, repay with a blessing." In his first letter to the Thessalonians Paul writes, "See that none of you repays evil for evil, but always seek to do good to one another and to all" (5:15). And in his letter to the Romans Paul writes, "Do not repay anyone evil for evil, but take thought for what is noble in the sight of all ... Never avenge yourselves" (Romans 12:17–18).

I find it undeniable that, in these passages, Jesus and the New Testament writers reject retribution. So how can it be that, in the face of the clear teaching of these passages, Christians over the centuries have nonetheless been defenders of retribution? They have commonly done so by using a line from Romans 12 to guide their interpretation of what Paul says in Romans 13.

In Romans 12, after telling his readers that they are not to "repay anyone evil for evil," Paul says, "for it is written, 'Vengeance is mine, I will repay, says the Lord'" (12: 19). Then, in the next chapter, Paul declares that governmental authorities are "God's servants," commissioned to exercise justice. The common interpretation of this declaration is that when governmental authorities punish wrongdoers, they are imposing retribution on God's behalf. It is on God's behalf, in God's stead, that they are wreaking vengeance—retribution, payback—on wrongdoers. When acting as private citizens, we are not to engage in retributive payback. When acting on God's behalf as a government official, one is authorized to exercise retribution.

My reply, which I have developed at some length in my book *Journey toward Justice*, goes as follows. The Greek word that Paul uses in chapter 12, which gets translated into English as "vengeance," is *ekdikēsis*. Paul does not use the word *ekdikēsis* in chapter 13, nor does he use the telltale word "repay." He does not say that the business of government is to exercise retribution—payback.

Neither does he say that governmental officials act on God's behalf—so that God acts by way of their acting. He says that governmental officials are *servants* of God. A servant of someone is not, as such, authorized to speak or act on behalf of his master.

In short, I regard the common interpretation of Romans 13 as unsupported by the text. Nowhere does Jesus or any New Testament writer say or suggest that when it comes to government officials, the negative side of the reciprocity code remains in effect. Do not repay evil for evil, says Jesus. Period. No exceptions.

Suppose, now, that we follow what I regard as the clear teaching of the New Testament and reject retribution. Does that mean that there is nothing intrinsically moral about punishment—that the decision whether or not to impose punishment depends entirely on its anticipated effects?

It does not. In recent years, some philosophers have introduced the idea of what they call the *expressive* theory of punishment. The idea is that when society, by way of its officials, punishes someone for an infraction, this should be understood as society forcefully expressing its condemnation of the person for what he did, forcefully *reproving* him or her, forcefully reprimanding them, forcefully declaring that what they did was wrong. In my book *Justice in Love* I proposed calling this the "reprobative" theory of punishment, on the ground that what is being expressed by the hard treatment is reproval. Compare a parent's punishment of a child. When a parent punishes a child for some infraction of the family's rules, the parent is not exercising retribution, payback. Or if he is, the relation of the parent to the child is extremely disturbed. The parent is reproving the child, forcefully declaring that what the child did was wrong. The parent also hopes that the punishment will have the effect of reforming the child. But apart from that hoped-for effect, the punishment consists, *as such*, of reproving the child. Unlike reformation of the wrongdoer, reproval is not a *causal consequence* of the punishment. To punish *just* is to reprove. In that way, punishment is an *intrinsically* moral activity.

Every society has a moral code to be followed by its members. One does not discern the moral code of a society by observing how its members do in fact act—all too often they act in violation of the code. One discerns a society's moral code by observing the social practice of members issuing moral directives to each other and the social practice of members praising and reproving each other. And one discerns how seriously the society regards a certain sort of infraction by observing how forcefully it expresses its condemnation, its reproval, of forbidden behavior.

I suggest that what makes just punishment an intrinsically moral activity, and not merely an activity that may or may not have good consequences for the wrongdoer or for society, is that it is society's way of forcefully reproving wrongdoers, and that, as such, it is an aspect—an indispensable aspect—of how a society upholds its moral code.

In the Old Testament/Hebrew Bible book of Leviticus we find a long list of examples of loving one's neighbor. The list concludes as follows: "you shall reprove your neighbor, or you will incur guilt yourself. You shall not take vengeance or bear a grudge against any of your people, but you shall love your neighbor as yourself" (19:17–18, NRSV).

This is striking. Reproving your neighbor, when he or she engages in wrongdoing, is an example of loving your neighbor; to fail to reprove your neighbor is to "incur guilt yourself." Consider the parent who never reproves her child for anything the child does. She may praise the child now and then; but she never reproves him for wrongdoing, neither verbally nor with some form of punishment. That is a wronging of the child, for which the parent "incurs guilt."

Back to where these reflections began. I think I understand, Kurt, why working to restore some malfunctioning system and to rebuild trust in that system sometimes feels in tension with doing what one can to see to it that wrongdoers are punished. But I hope these reflections on punishment have made clear that, whatever tensions one may feel in one's day-to-day pursuit of these two activities, in principle they not only fit together but are interlocked—provided one does not think of punishment as retribution but as reproval.

One of the systems in Honduras that ASJ is working to restore is the criminal justice system. That system will not be restored merely by the enactment of good laws—though of course that is necessary. It will be restored only when criminals are apprehended and forcefully but justly reproved for that they have done. When that happens, trust in the system will also be restored. It all fits together.

Your friend,
Nick

12

Love and Repentance

Dear Nick,

Thank you for these insightful reflections on reproval and the role of retributive and restorative justice. I found especially important your distinction between punishment understood as retribution and punishment understood as the expression of disapproval; and I believe you are right that Scripture rejects retribution. As Christians, our desire should not be for "eye for an eye" payback, but a commitment to social reproval of wrong behavior.

Your letter has made me spend some time reflecting on what should empower and drive us to reprove our authorities—first, a desire for their repentance and transformation, and second, a love "beyond fear," both for those closest to us in our own lives but also for everyone as a beloved child of God, even our enemies or those authorities with whom we deeply disagree. I want to tell three stories that I think illustrate these key points.

First, I think the biblical story of King David and the prophet Nathan is a good example of what a loving but corrective reproach can look like.

From the moment David spies Bathsheba bathing, he is determined to have her, against her will, against the law, and against God's commandments. He involves his whole court in facilitating his illegal and sinful desires; he dictates military strategy to kill an officer in order to cover up his sin. He leaves Bathsheba pregnant, and her husband, Uriah, dead.

The prophet Nathan comes in the aftermath of this chaos and requests a meeting with David. He tells the following story:

"There were two men in a certain town, one rich and the other poor. ²The rich man had a very large number of sheep and cattle, ³but the poor man had nothing except one little ewe lamb he had bought. He raised it, and it grew up with him and his children. It shared his food, drank from his cup and even slept in his arms. It was like a daughter to him.

⁴"Now a traveler came to the rich man, but the rich man refrained from taking one of his own sheep or cattle to prepare a meal for the traveler who had come to him. Instead, he took the ewe lamb that belonged to the poor man and prepared it for the one who had come to him."

⁵David burned with anger against the man and said to Nathan, "As surely as the LORD lives, the man who did this must die! ⁶He must pay for that lamb four times over, because he did such a thing and had no pity."

⁷Then Nathan said to David, "You are the man!"

(2 Samuel 12:1–7)

This rebuke hits David in the heart. It cuts through his selfishness and thoughtlessness so that he repents of the evil he has done and prostrates himself before the Lord. We do not know if his repentance included reparations to Bathsheba, but we do know he acknowledged his sin and sought forgiveness. He spent six days fasting, sleeping in sackcloth, and crying out to God.

When I read this story, I thought about which of the story's characters I most identified with: David, Nathan, or the people of David's court who supported and facilitated David's actions.

I knew I didn't want to be like David. He did horrific things, committing rape and murder, both sinning and lying to cover up his sin. This seems to put him in a different category from most of us; but really, we are not so different. We may never kill another person, but we regularly use our words as weapons and treat others with contempt.

Despite David's actions, he can also serve as an example for us. He sinned horribly, but also repented passionately. When was the last time you spent an hour crying out in repentance to God, let alone six days? I can't think of a time in my own life. I'm more likely to hear people recount sin or cruelty with a shrug—laughing about how they "told off" a mistaken waiter or charged expensive dragon fruit as bananas at their local self-checkout.

In his repentance, David represents both a high and a low in our relationship with God. The members of David's court, by contrast, represent the status quo. They are not prominent characters in the story. The dozens of soldiers, servants, and courtesans that inhabited David's court are neither named nor noticeable. Yet the members of the court must have seen Bathsheba brought to the palace, or even helped to do it. Surely word traveled. Everyone saw Uriah sleeping on the castle steps even as Bathsheba's dresses stretched tighter. Uriah's entire battalion had to be told to step back and leave him fighting alone; they all followed their orders.

I may be drawn to Nathan's boldness or David's repentance, but I think most of us in our daily lives are more like people of the court. We see those with power acting with impunity and choose to do nothing. Our boss mistreats one of our coworkers—we decide we don't want to get into it. An acquaintance tells an offensive joke—we laugh uncomfortably and say nothing. We hear about abuse, embezzlement, injustice, and we satisfy ourselves by thinking that we would never do such a thing ourselves—in the process, acting in a way that allows the corruption and abuse of power to continue.

What would it look like instead to live like Nathan? When I read this story I want to be like Nathan, and I think most people would agree, sharing a desire to boldly speak truth to power. Nathan went before the king with a message of reckoning for his sins—prophets of God had been killed for less. We may say we want to do the same, but do we, really? When we look back over our last week or year, have we done anything remotely similar? Few of us are willing to face the consequences of standing up to abusers in even petty incidences, let alone in situations of life or death.

I think we can learn from Nathan's bravery, but also from his tact.

Nathan is a prophet of God, but he also has a relationship with David—he knows how to tug on David's heartstrings and get him to listen. Nathan wants to speak truth, but more than that, he wants David to repent and change. Therefore, he doesn't picket outside the castle condemning David; he goes inside, and starts with a story. Only when they had established common ground ("*David burned with anger*") does Nathan tell the truth he had come to share—"*You are that man.*"

This approach is what causes David to realize: "I have sinned against the LORD."

Then, perhaps even more remarkably, Nathan replies: "The LORD has taken away your sin. You are not going to die (2 Samuel 12:13)."

I think this extension of forgiveness is almost as bold as decrying David's sin in the first place. If I had been in Nathan's shoes, knowing everything that David did, I would have wanted punishment, not repentance. Of course, David does still suffer the consequences of his sin, including war, familial infighting, and the death of his and Bathsheba's child. But despite all that, I think it's difficult to be open to forgiveness, repentance, and change from authorities for whom we want revenge and punishment.

Nathan's attitude is very different from another biblical character, Jonah. God calls Jonah to preach repentance to Nineveh, but Jonah doesn't want to—he boards a boat instead in a fruitless attempt to flee God. Many are familiar with the story that follows—how Jonah's boat faces a fierce storm, and he convinces the sailors to throw him overboard, where a giant fish swallows him. After three days, the fish spits him out onto dry land, and he goes at long last to Nineveh.

But the story doesn't end there. After confronting the people of Nineveh with their sin, they actually repent wholeheartedly. Like David, they fast, put on sackcloth, and turn from their evil ways. In the end, God spares their lives: "But to Jonah, this seemed very wrong, and he became angry . . . 'LORD, take away my life,'" he says, "For it is better for me to die than to live (Jonah 4:1, 3)."

Nathan confronted David with his sin, but more than that, he called him to repent and change. David's repentance is good for David, but also good for the people of his kingdom. Jonah, by contrast, only wants to preach punishment. When the people of Nineveh repent, which is surely the best thing for them and their community, he responds petulantly. He had wanted to watch Nineveh's total destruction.

Reproval cannot be made from a position of vengeance—your previous letter points out that reproval, instead, is part of loving our neighbors. Yet even when we do stand up for what's right, how often are we like Jonah? As much as we welcome grace for our own failures, we want vengeance, not repentance from abusive bosses or corrupt politicians, even if a change of heart would be best for both authorities and the people that they govern.

I have already written about how justice work requires the bravery of a prophetic voice, but when I think about applying this to my own life, the piece I haven't discussed yet is love. One of my favorite verses in the Bible, 1 John 4:18, says: *"There is no fear in love. But perfect love drives out fear ..."*

I want to tell a final story that I think illustrates this. Jo Ann and I raised our children in a rough neighborhood. There is a gang presence, and one or two murders every month. We love our community, but still, when my oldest daughter Anna was a teenager, I would always walk her to the church youth group that met a few blocks away.

Even when walking with me, Anna would sometimes get comments or catcalls from the neighborhood boys. One of the most common (and most infuriating) was actually directed at me: *"Suegro!"* the boys would shout, "Hey, father-in-law!"

This always made me tense up, and because I would do anything to protect my daughter, I would start to imagine scenarios of how I would protect her. I know that if one of those boys had ever tried something, I would have done anything to protect her, even if there were a lot of them, even if they were armed. In that moment, I wouldn't think about the consequences for me—I love my daughter, and that love is stronger than any fear I would feel under those circumstances.

You, I'm sure, can imagine this love. Imagine, Nick, if your granddaughters were spending some time with us in Nueva Suyapa and I was showing them around the neighborhood. Imagine that a group of these guys went after them. I know you would want me to do everything in my power to protect them.

It's easy for my mind to make the connection between fearlessly loving my own daughter, and protecting the daughter or granddaughter of a friend like you. But we both know that *every single person* in our communities is someone's son or daughter; every single parent hopes that their own children will be protected and saved. What's more, every one of us is a child of God, equally loved and equally deserving of that same protection.

"Should I not have compassion on the great city of Nineveh?" (Jonah 4:11) God asks Jonah. God loved Nineveh and its people, despite their sin, just as God loved David despite the evil he had done. He wanted repentance—both for David and Nineveh's own good and for what transformation would mean for those entire kingdoms.

However hard it may be to imagine, God loves the politicians who are profiting from corruption, just as God loves corruption's most marginalized victims. God wants repentance, a change of heart and action, even of the authorities who are stealing money from programs for the poor and abusing human rights. I think this must impact how we approach advocacy.

Love, as we've said, does not erase consequences. Authorities should still pay for their sinful or illegal actions. But I do think approaching advocacy from a posture of love must change our expectations. Do we believe that God can work change in the hardest hearts? Are we actually open to repentance or even reconciliation if that change occurs?

So many people in society are like Jonah, calling out authorities with righteous anger and filling their conversations or social media posts with hate and condemnation. Others are like the people of David's court, whispering among themselves about atrocities that are occurring, but preferring to stay out of the way. I think we all need to be more like Nathan, looking for the right strategy that will bring home to members of government or other authorities that they need to repent and change their hearts and actions.

I believe that perfect love, fearless love, can sometimes mean loving victims through the process of arresting, reproving, and challenging those who do them harm. But I believe that it can also mean loving perpetrators by being prophetic voices like Nathan to David, laying their sin clearly before them and hoping for their repentance. Here at ASJ we want to love our neighbors in both of these ways.

Your friend,
Kurt

13

Evoking the Emotions of Empathy and Anger

Dear Kurt,

In our conversations with each other you told me that it was especially the murder of Dionisio that led you to reflect on the role of forgiveness, punishment, restoration, etc. in the work of ASJ. At one point
you asked me whether I thought there was space for what you called
"healthy anger" in justice work. That question reminded me of my own
reflections on my experience in South Africa and my engagement with
Palestinians, reflections which led me to conclude that there is not only
space for healthy anger in justice work. Justice work requires anger—
and more generally, requires emotional engagement with perpetrators
and victims, both on the part of those who work directly for justice and
on the part of members of the public. Being informed about the issues
is not enough. Emotional engagement is necessary.

After my visit to South Africa in 1975 and my meeting with Palestinians on the west side of Chicago in 1978—encounters that I described in my second letter—I found myself reflecting on why I was
so moved by these experiences whereas, though I had actively participated in the civil rights movement in the US and in opposition to the
Vietnam War, nothing that I experienced in those two movements
had affected me in the same way. Why the difference?

The answer I eventually arrived at was that, in these two awakenings, I had seen the faces and heard the voices of the wronged,
whereas that was not the case, or was only barely the case, for my
participation in the civil rights movement and in my opposition to
the Vietnam War.

And what was it about seeing the faces and hearing the voices of those victims of injustice that moved me to speak up for them?

The answer I settled on was that seeing the faces and hearing the voices of the wronged evoked empathy in me. By "empathy" I do not mean compassion, and even less do I mean pity. I did feel compassion. But the compassion was enveloped in empathy. I found myself empathetically united with these people, emotionally identified with them. I felt anger with their anger, hurt with their hurt, humiliation with their humiliation.

The same thing happened to me during my first visit to Honduras, in that small living room that I wrote about in my previous letter, when two mothers described the rape of their daughters and spoke of the refusal of the police to investigate until ASJ intervened. Here, too, seeing the faces and hearing the voices of the wronged evoked empathy in me.

Perhaps some people are motivated to engage in the struggle for justice by a sense of duty. Perhaps some are motivated by the conviction that this is what a good and virtuous person does. And perhaps some are motivated by the conviction that, in so acting, they are obeying God. But in my case, I did not really get involved until my emotions were engaged—until I cared. I doubt that I am peculiar in this respect. I think that, for most people, being motivated to struggle for the righting of injustice requires emotional engagement.

I remember discussing the role of empathy in the struggle for justice with you and your staff on my second visit to Honduras, and using my own case as an example. Carlos Hernandez was in the audience. He reported that he had just come back from a meeting in which he found himself seated across the table from a man who, almost certainly, had been one of the brains behind the murder of Dionisio. Carlos reported feeling anger welling up within him at this man who was still free to perpetrate his foul deeds, and finding himself more determined than ever to see that he was convicted of his crimes.

His remark made me realize that, in my own case, too, there was anger at the perpetrators. Empathy with the victims was dominant, since it was their faces I had seen and their voices I had heard. But anger was there, in the background. Carlos's experience was the reverse of mine. It was the face and voice of the perpetrator that confronted him, so anger was his dominant emotion. But, of course, he also felt empathy with all those who were joined with him in grieving Dionisio's murder.

What I take away from my reflection on these experiences, Kurt, is the principle that, for most people, serious commitment to the struggle for justice requires emotional engagement in the form of empathy with the victims and anger at the perpetrators. One's experience may cause one or the other of these to be dominant; but both will be involved. No doubt there will always be other emotions involved as well. But I have come to think that these two—empathy with the victims and anger at the perpetrators—are, as it were, the emotional foundation of the struggle for justice. What this implies for the work of ASJ and similar organizations is that they cannot just dispense information; they have to engage people's emotions.

Though in my case it was actually seeing the faces and hearing the voices of the wronged that evoked my empathy, and though in Carlos's case it was actually seeing the face and hearing the voice of one of the perpetrators that evoked his anger, it's clear that one doesn't have to be face to face with victims for empathy to be evoked, or face to face with perpetrators for anger to be evoked. Film can work just as powerfully, as can drama and fiction. Witness the powerful effect on nineteenth-century readers of *Uncle Tom's Cabin*. On the other hand, it is my impression that journalistic reports seldom have the same effect. Why the difference?

I think the difference is that when we actually see the faces and hear the voices, or see and hear them on film, or meet them in drama or fiction, we don't just receive information but we imagine what it's like to be persons of that sort in that sort of situation. It is this *imagining what it's like* that evokes empathy or anger. Journalism seldom evokes this sort of imagining. I don't claim that it cannot. Just that usually it doesn't.

There's another difference between Carlos's experience and mine that is worth taking note of. I was not myself a victim of South African apartheid, nor was I a Palestinian victim of Israeli oppression. I was, instead, an onlooker to these two cases of social injustice—an onlooker who, as a result of my awakenings, became a supporter of the movements to eliminate these injustices. Carlos, by contrast, was himself a victim of the injustice perpetrated by the man sitting across the table from him. He was one of those cast into grief by Dionisio's murder.

That difference between our two cases suggests the following thought: the participants in most social justice movements are a blend of victims and supporters of the victims. I have been a supporter-participant in the anti-apartheid movement in South Africa and in the anti-Israeli-oppression movement in Palestine. Carlos has been and is a victim-participant in some, at least, of the social justice crusades in Honduras.

Confronted with social injustice, typically there are non-victim members of the public who are angry with the perpetrators and feel empathy for the victims before any social justice movement gets under way. And—more surprisingly—often a good many of the victims harbor no particular anger toward their victimizers and no particular empathy for their fellow victims. They are resigned to their condition. There's nothing to be done, they think; so why get all stirred up? Or they have internalized the attitude of their oppressors toward them: they deserve their fate. Or this is their God-ordained place in the social order; it would be wrong to resist.

The moral is that, for both victims and potential supporters, social justice movements must blend tapping into emotions of empathy and anger already present, with evoking those emotions in those who do not yet experience them. It is no accident that a prominent component in the denunciations of injustice by the prophets of ancient Israel was the forceful expression of anger. Here is just one example of many:

Ah, you who make iniquitous decrees,
   who write oppressive statutes,
   to turn aside the need from justice,
   and to rob the poor of my people of their right,
   that widows may be your spoil,
   and that you may make the orphans your prey.

(Isa 10:1–2)

71

I suggested that the emotions of empathy and anger, in victims and supporters, are a necessary ingredient of social justice movements. It's important to note that empathy with the victims is not, by itself, sufficient; there must also be anger at the perpetrators. Which presupposes, of course, that the perpetrators must be identified as such. Empathy with the victims in the absence of anger at the perpetrators evokes charity, benevolence, relief—or hand-wringing. We see photos of pitiful looking orphans in Haiti. We are touched. We send a contribution for the alleviation of their plight to the charitable organization whose name appears below the photos. We feel no anger, only empathy. We do not ask whether these orphans are the victims of injustice.

In short, social justice movements and organizations cannot limit themselves to evoking empathy with suffering people. They have to make clear that these people are suffering because they are being wronged. They are not victims of some natural disaster; they are victims of injustice. The perpetrators have to be identified and condemned. This is the point at which information and social analysis become relevant. In one of your previous letters you describe very lucidly the ASJ model for accomplishing these things. This is also the point at which a new form of anger typically enters the picture—anger by the perpetrators at those who identify and condemn them as perpetrators.

Some truly lamentable dynamics of human nature come into view when we take note of the need for emotional engagement in social justice movements. Empathy with the wronged was evoked in me by the three encounters I have described. But it was not evoked in the Afrikaners who spoke up at the conference in defense of apartheid, even though they had seen the faces and heard the voices of the people of color in South Africa far more often than I had. It was not evoked, and it is not evoked, in most Israelis, even though they see the faces and hear the voices of Palestinians far more often than I have. It was not evoked in those who abused, and in those who tolerated the abuse of, the children and mothers of Tegucigalpa, even though their contact with those children and mothers was far more frequent than mine. It was not evoked in the slaveholders of nineteenth century America, even though they saw the faces and heard the voices of the slaves far more often and directly than did the readers of *Uncle Tom's Cabin*. In all these cases, empathy was blocked—blocked by the hardening of the heart.

The causes of the hardening of the heart, and of the resultant blocking of empathy, are multiple. Let me briefly mention a few of the most common causes.

One reason why empathy is often blocked is that the hard-hearted person has learned to dehumanize the victims—or if not precisely to dehumanize them, to think of them as lesser human beings with diminished sensibilities, sometimes even as loathsome. They are vermin, scum, terrorists.

A second reason why empathy is often blocked is that those whose hearts are hardened have embraced a narrative that says the plight of the victims is their own fault. The Palestinians, it is said, fled their villages of their own accord in 1948 and continue to refuse to negotiate with Israel in good faith because they continue to refuse to recognize the legitimacy of the State of Israel. Their plight is of their own making. Empathy is out of order. Another example: the poor, it is often said, are poor because they are lazy; their poverty is their own fault.

A third reason why empathy is often blocked is that the hard-hearted have embraced an ideology that says some great good will be achieved by the present policies. Securing that great good comes at the cost of the suffering of some, and that's unfortunate. But the great good to be achieved will outweigh the present suffering. So one must harden one's heart and do what the great good requires. Pol Pot preached to his followers in Cambodia that they must rid themselves of emotion and become purely rational.

There is yet a fourth reason why empathy is often blocked, and this is perhaps the most common of all. Empathy for the victims is blocked by the person's realization that feeling empathy would lead to acknowledging his own complicity in the plight of the victims. Acknowledging that complicity would require reforming his way of life; and he finds that such reform is more than he can bring himself to do. He would be ostracized by friends, make less money, lose his position of privilege and power. Best, then, to harden one's heart and make contributions every now and then to charitable organizations. Then nothing has to change.

To evoke empathy for the victims, and thus to advance the cause of justice, one has to diagnose the hardening of the heart in the case one is dealing with, and then do what one can to remove that cause. In each case, one has to craft one's approach to one's diagnosis of what it is that is causing the blocking of empathy. A number of Israeli historians have shown that the standard Israeli narrative, which says that the plight of the Palestinians is of their own making, is simply false.

Sad to say, attempts to remove blockages to empathy are often unsuccessful; then pressure of one kind or another has to be applied. That's what happened in the case of South Africa. It was the boycotts that eventually had an effect. In his fine book *Blessed Are the Organized*, Jeffrey Stout describes a number of cases in the US in which justice was eventually achieved by bringing pressure of one sort or another to bear on the perpetrators.

You asked whether there is "space for healthy anger in justice work." If my observations in this letter are correct, then not only is there space for healthy anger in justice work; justice work cannot succeed without healthy anger. The struggle for justice requires, in those working for justice, healthy anger against the perpetrators of injustice and healthy empathy for the victims.

Your friend,
Nick

14

The Assassination of the "Lawyer for the Poor"

Dear Nick,

Thank you for your letter, in which you tacitly grant me "permission" to feel anger about losses such as the tragic murder of Dionisio, who was, and continues to be, one of my heroes. I'm definitely not a philosopher, but I have spent a lot of time thinking about the role of justice, forgiveness, and repentance in Dionisio's murder. I'll share my thoughts here and I look forward to reading your response.

One of ASJ's early projects was working to ensure that security guards and cleaning women received at least the legal minimum wage, along with all the benefits that they deserved. Security guards and cleaning women in Honduras are some of the poorest working people, and companies take advantage of their desperation. They are commonly asked to work seventy to eighty hours a week, while receiving as little as half of the minimum wage. Many of them get no vacation time and no health care; uniforms and materials are deducted from their paycheck—all of which is illegal.

Not only was this a glaring injustice, it was extremely common. While Honduras had a police force of just over 10,000, more than 75,000 private security guards protected homes, neighborhoods, and businesses. Large companies contracted out thousands of cleaning staff to work in malls, grocery stores, offices, and even hospitals and government institutions.

We thought, and still do, that one way to help the poor and their families was to make sure they earned at least the minimum wage required by law, which in 2005 was just under $100 per month. Dionisio represented guards and cleaners, fighting to get them that minimum pay. Several companies seemed cooperative at first; but as our case moved through the courts, they started getting nervous and we began to receive anonymous threats. Our lawsuit was hitting these companies where it hurt—their profit margins.

Dionisio truly believed in this cause. He was one of the kindest people I have known, and cared deeply about the people he worked to defend. I remember asking him about his weekend one Monday morning, when he told me that one of the security guards he was representing had been forced to move with his family to a cheaper apartment. Dionisio not only lent him his truck to make the move; he spent the weekend moving heavy boxes and helping them settle in.

Dionisio was killed on a Monday morning. We had just finished our weekly staff devotions where I had sat next to him, and we prayed together. Afterwards, he left to go to the court to follow up on the case against the security guard company. While he waited in traffic just a few yards from the courthouse, a motorcycle with two masked men pulled up next to him, fired a spray of bullets through the window, and then sped away. Dionisio died instantly.

When I got the call a few minutes later, it seemed impossible to believe. I remember calling his wife to tell her what had happened. They had a six-year-old son, Mauricio. I remember telling the staff. But all along, I remember thinking that it had to be a mistake. We had just been praying together. In the days that followed, the whole staff was heartbroken. We had often joked about being David up against Goliath; but until then, I don't think we realized the size of the giants we were up against.

The next weeks were a scary time. A few days after Dionisio's murder, Carlos was chased by a masked man on a motorcycle. We worried about our staff, almost all women, and whether they could withstand the atmosphere of fear that our enemies had created.

While those initial weeks were full of fear, ultimately, Dionisio's murder served to strengthen our resolve. Far from quitting, our staff threw themselves into their work. We hired a lawyer and an investigator especially to work on Dionisio's murder case. We continued our labor rights project, refusing to let Dionisio's killers get the last word.

Beyond sorrow, the emotion I most remember from this period is anger. I desperately wanted justice for Dionisio, and maybe even revenge, retribution. At the same time, I was bothered by doubts about how I, a Christian, should respond to this horrific event. Should I extend forgiveness to Dionisio's killers? Should we ask for a meeting with the executives of the firm we were convinced had put out the hit on him? When suspects were eventually arrested, would people expect us to make a statement? Should we say we forgave them? Was it OK that I wanted the suspects to face the strongest penalties the law allowed?

I know you're the philosopher of the two of us, but in this letter I want to write to you about what I've learned about forgiveness as I've worked through Dionisio's death.

We are taught, especially in the church, of the power of forgiveness. I understood theoretically that it was something we were supposed to do. But the hit men who were eventually arrested denied the murder. It took us almost four years to get a conviction in the case; but while we were eventually able to get the hit men sent to jail, the executives of the security guard company, who we were sure had hired them, never faced any consequences at all. They were never apprehended, never punished. Nor was there any expression of guilt. So what was the place of forgiveness in this case? Did it have a place?

I recently saw a photo series of victims of the Rwandan genocide posing for photographs with the people who were responsible for their pain. In one remarkable image, a man and a woman stand side by side in what appears to be an old schoolhouse. They are holding hands.

"The day I thought of asking pardon, I felt unburdened and relieved. I had lost my humanity because of the crime I committed, but now I am like any human being," says the man, Dominique Ndahimana. The woman, Cansilde Munganyika, responds: "After I was chased from my village and Dominique and others looted it, I became homeless and insane. Later, when he asked my pardon, I said: 'I have nothing to feed my children. Are you going to help raise my children? Are you going to build a house for them?' The next week, Dominique came with some survivors and former prisoners who had perpetrated genocide. There were more than fifty of them, and they built my family a house. Ever since then, I have started to feel better. I was like a dry stick; now I feel peaceful in my heart, and I share this peace with my neighbors."

This is restorative justice at its best. The hurt is acknowledged, and also addressed. Dominique offers Cansilde more than an apology, he helps her reconstruct her life. She grants forgiveness. In the process they both feel healed.

Dionisio's case was not like this. In fact, few cases in Honduras are. Gang members kill neighbors or ex-girlfriends and brag about it. Corrupt officials pocket millions, and then deny or even justify their actions. In these cases, can forgiveness happen without repentance? Can there be reconciliation?

Forgiveness with Repentance

In the aftermath of the Rwandan genocide, or in the well-known biblical stories of Peter, Paul, David, or the prodigal son, forgiveness only occurs after the perpetrators humble themselves and ask for it. The perpetrator's change of heart is what allows both the victim and the perpetrator to heal.

In these cases, forgiveness has benefits for both the perpetrator and the wronged. The perpetrator's apology helps the wronged person see them as human, and to open up their heart, letting go of anger and hatred that might have been building up. The perpetrator, on the other hand, absolves some of the intense guilt he may feel, restores broken relationships, and reinforces his own "humanness."

For this apology to be meaningful, however, it must accompany repentance, which is not the same as regret. A man who beats his wife may follow his aggression with apologies, affection, and promises to change; but the real test occurs when his anger flares a few weeks later. What's more, forgiveness does not preclude consequences. The wife who was beaten may extend forgiveness to her husband; at the same time, she may still report him to the police.

Justice demands consequences, or punishment, as you write. A woman who persistently speeds or drives drunk is acting in a way that puts herself and others around her at risk. If an initial ticket is not enough to dissuade her from this behavior, she may lose her driving license after a subsequent offense, or eventually spend time in jail. Her punishment functions both to express society's reproval of what she has done and to protect the public from danger.

God forgave David for his horrific actions towards Bathsheba and Uriah; nonetheless, David was not allowed to build God's temple, reaffirming how contrary murder and sexual violence are to God's kingdom. David's sin was not forgotten. Nor is "forgetting" the purpose of forgiveness, particularly when we have lost someone we love. Our goal isn't to erase our memories, but to separate the bitterness from them.

Forgiveness without Repentance

Forgiveness in response to repentance is one way to move past bitterness, but it is not the only way. Another way that people find healing is through the appropriate exercise of second-order corrective (criminal) justice. When we work with a family who have lost their husband and father to gang violence, they almost always feel a sense of closure and even of peace when the perpetrator is finally sentenced to prison, even if he goes away remorseless.

We can even imagine that family visiting the prison and extending to the gunman their willingness to forgive. If he is not open to repentance, he won't benefit, but the family will as they symbolically release their anger and desire for revenge. It's still a risk—maybe the family will be mocked or laughed at, maybe they'll stir up negative emotions. But just maybe, the perpetrator will be touched, opening the door for future change. It will at least help the family move forward in healing.

ASJ worked a few years ago with an eight-year-old girl who had been repeatedly abused by her father. With our help, the father was arrested and sent to prison, and our psychologists worked extensively with the young girl. After a few months of therapy, she said that she wanted to write her father a letter: "I feel really bad because of what you did to me," said the letter, which she showed to her counselor, "I forgive you ... but I hope you don't continue in these bad things because if you keep doing bad things, you are going back to jail." This young girl's forgiveness didn't require her father's repentance, nor did it preclude consequences. In fact, it was only possible in a context where punishment, in this case, the arrest of the father, had occurred.

No Repentance, No Justice

After the death of Dionisio, we found ourselves in an even more diffi-cult situation than the previous two. In a case where there is neither repentance nor the exercise of criminal justice, what would forgive-ness look like? Jesus on the cross called out—"Father, forgive them, for they know not what they do." I struggled to understand how that example applied to us.

In difficult cases like these, I think we need to do three things. The first is not to resign ourselves to the lack of criminal justice, but to continue to work towards that end. The men who killed Dionisio needed to face consequences for their actions. Those consequences need not be violent or vengeful; but they are needed as a way of de-claring the value of Dionisio's life, and the lives of everyone else who might fall victim as long as the perpetrators remained free.

The second thing I think we need to do, even in the absence of repentance or punishment, is to let go of our hatred, our anger, and our desire for revenge. In the years after Dionisio's death, the idea of taking matters into my own hands would regularly enter my mind. I could have carried out some sort of vigilante justice; but in pursuing a twisted and consuming personal quest for revenge, I would have been the one who suffered. Those who let anger and bitterness rule their lives have been doubly victimized. I've heard it said that holding on to hatred is like drinking poison and waiting for the other person to die. The consciences of those hit men may be untroubled by the evil they did, but if I pursued revenge, I would become more and more full of the poison of hatred. Then, not only would they have killed Dionisio, they would also have stolen some of the best parts of me.

The third thing I think we need to do is to avoid dehumanization of the culprits, writing them off as hopeless causes. If one day they face legal consequences or seek forgiveness, I don't want to be so hardened towards them that I reject the possibility of mutual healing. No matter how despicable or hardened people seem in their ways, our belief in the redeeming power of Christ must leave some hope for change. We should not forget that all of us are loved and cherished by God. We also should not forget that all of us are subject to our sinful natures; all of us have made mistakes.

Again, forgiving someone does not mean that there will be no punishment for their actions. Jesus' death on the cross was a tragic consequence of our own actions. With his dying words Jesus granted forgiveness to the very people who were torturing him. Whether they accepted that forgiveness was up to them; whether we accept his forgiveness is up to us. For us to heal, we must be willing to let our own hearts change, to "go and sin no more," and address and make right the consequences of our angry words, our pain-causing actions, and even our sinful thoughts.

As we heal our hearts with God, we can then think about extending similar forgiveness to others. Part of our practical work is to seek justice, both first-order and second-order justice, both ensuring that people face punishment for their harmful crimes and working towards a society in which people's safety and dignity are no longer violated. At the same time, part of our spiritual work is to ensure that our hearts are in the right place to release hatred and anger, and maybe, if the other party's heart is open, to seek out reconciliation.

So, many years after our initial conversation, I wonder how you would respond to these conclusions. Would you offer any additional recommendations? When I think about the factors that motivate ASJ's actions, much of it stems from outrage at the ways people have been oppressed and marginalized? How can we also incorporate a Christ-like forgiveness into our work? How might we balance the pursuit of criminal convictions with the desire not to dehumanize others or be consumed by hatred?

Your friend,
Kurt

15

Punishment and Forgiveness

Dear Kurt,

Clearly the issue of when to forgive is one that you in ASJ have thought about a lot. You report that, in your own case, it was especially your anger at the murder of Dionisio that led you to raise questions about the role of forgiveness, punishment, restoration, etc., in the work of ASJ. I judge that it will advance our thinking together about these rather complicated matters if, in this letter, I first do "the philosopher's thing" of standing back and reflecting on the nature and scope of forgiveness, and then reflect on the relation of forgiveness to punishment.

There can be no doubt that forgiveness is an important component in the way of life that Jesus taught his followers and that the writers of the New Testament epistles taught their readers. A persistent point of controversy, however, is over the intended scope of the injunction to forgive: are we each to forgive whoever wrongs us, and for whatever wrongs they do to us?

It's commonly said that it is indeed the intended scope of the New Testament injunction to forgive. However, I know of no passage in Scripture which says or suggests that one should forgive in the absence of repentance. Luke reports Jesus as saying, on one occasion, "If another disciple sins, you must rebuke the offender, and if there is repentance, you must forgive. And if the same person sins against you seven times a day, and turns back to you seven times and says, 'I repent, you must forgive'" (Luke 17:3-4, NRSV). In Matthew's narration, Peter seems to have found this teaching incredible. So, to check

82

out whether Jesus really meant to say what he did say, Peter asks, "Lord, if another member of the church sins against me, how often should I forgive? As many as seven times?" Jesus' response is hyperbolic: "Not seven times, but, I tell you, seventy-seven times" (Matt 18:21-22, NRSV). In other words: forgive as often as the wrongdoer repents. Jesus instructs us to love our enemies—our enemies being those who have wronged us and are unrepentant. Jesus does not instruct us to *forgive* our enemies.

Rather often, when I have given a public talk in which I argued that nowhere in Scripture is it said or suggested that we should forgive in the absence of repentance, someone objects by citing the cry of Jesus on the cross concerning those who are crucifying him: "Father, forgive them, for they do not know what they are doing." I submit that this is a mistranslation of the Greek. If someone doesn't realize that what they have done is wrong (and if their ignorance is not culpable), one doesn't forgive them; one excuses them. The Greek term in Luke 23:24 that is usually translated into English as "forgive" has, as its root meaning, the more general idea of *passing over*: It applies to both forgiving and excusing. "Father, pass over what they have done, for they do not know what they are doing." (In your previous letter, Kurt, you used the familiar translation, "Father, forgive them...")

The point, the goal, of forgiveness is reconciliation between wrongdoer and victim. But if there is no repentance by the wrongdoer, there can be no reconciliation. That's why Jesus and the writers of the New Testament epistles do not enjoin forgiveness in the absence of repentance.

What, then, is forgiveness? The goal of forgiveness, to say it again, is reconciliation. But what is the thing itself? Entire books have been written in answer to this question, developing many different understandings. Here is obviously not the place to delve into that literature. Let me just state, compactly, my own understanding. Forgiveness, as I understand it, consists of *not holding against the wrongdoer what he did to one*. By "not holding it against him" I mean: not regarding it as a blotch on his moral character. He did it. It was wrong. I remember that he did it. But he has repented. Morally speaking, he is no longer the same person that he was. So in weighing up his moral character as a whole, I no longer regard what he did to me as a blotch on his moral character. I no longer count it against him I treat him in the same way as I would if I *excused* him for what he did. (I develop this understanding of forgiveness at some length in my *Justice in Love*).

Parenthetically, I should note that, in these comments about the nature of forgiveness, I have in mind the use of the term "forgiveness" that one finds in Scripture and in the philosophical and theological literature. I well remember the occasion on which I gave a talk on the nature of forgiveness in which I assumed that forgiveness aims at reconciliation, and hence presupposes repentance, and someone in the question period afterward declaring forcefully, with an expression of extreme perplexity on her face, "Forgiveness has nothing to do with the wrongdoer."

I was as perplexed by her declaration as she was perplexed by my talk. So I asked her to expand on what she had in mind. It turned out that she was a therapist and that, in the therapeutic literature, there is a quite different use of the term "forgiveness" from that in Scripture and in the philosophical and theological literature. Forgiveness, in the therapeutic literature, is aimed at controlling or eliminating the emotions stirred up in one by being wronged so that one can get on with one's life—no longer allowing the emotions evoked by the wrong done one to fester. Forgiveness, so understood, has nothing to do with reconciliation. The wrongdoer doesn't enter the picture. It's a purely internal act, not a relational engagement.

Looking back at your reflections in your last letter on the relevance of forgiveness when repentance is absent, I conclude, Kurt, that you were using the term "forgiveness" in a way somewhat different from its use in either the philosophical/theological tradition or the therapeutic tradition—and why not? You note that, in the absence of repentance, one can and should go beyond the interior work of getting one's emotions under control to seek just punishment of the wrongdoer, to resist dehumanizing him, to hold oneself open to the possibility of repentance and reconciliation, etc. These are not purely internal activities; they are *interpersonal*. And you suggest that

84

controlling one's emotions of anger, hatred, etc. is not only good for one's own mental health but morally required.

Back to forgiveness as understood in Scripture and in the philosophical and theological literature. What is the relation of forgiveness, so understood, to punishment? I recall, once again, the remark you once made to me, that a criticism ASJ sometimes gets from certain Christians in Honduras is that, as a Christian organization, it should be urging and practicing the forgiveness of wrongdoers rather than seeking their punishment. If there is to be punishment, let others see to it. The criticism assumes that urging and practicing forgiveness of wrongdoers is incompatible with seeking their punishment. Is that assumption correct?

We are all familiar with cases in which forgiveness of the repentant wrongdoer did include—and rightly so—refraining from punishing him and from seeking to have him punished. The writers of pagan antiquity taught that punishment of wrongdoers is morally required. I interpret Christian Scripture, in what it says about forgiveness, as teaching that it is sometimes morally appropriate to forgive the wrongdoer and not seek his or her punishment.

But does forgiveness *necessarily include* refraining from punishment and from seeking punishment? Is forgiveness incompatible with punishment? Might those Christian critics of ASJ be correct in assuming that practicing forgiveness is incompatible with seeking punishment?

Suppose we adopt, as I think we should, the reprobative or expressive rationale for punishment that I presented in a previous letter (letter #11). Punishment, so understood and practiced, is society's way of forcefully expressing its condemnation of what was done; it is society's way of reproving the wrongdoer. Hasn't punishment, so understood, lost its point if the wrongdoer has repented of what he did? In repenting, the wrongdoer condemns *himself* for what he did. Is there any point in society also expressing its condemnation? Isn't this just "piling on"?

Not necessarily. Punishment may retain its relevance. The point of society forcefully expressing its condemnation of what the wrongdoer did is not to persuade the wrongdoer that what he did was wrong—though it may have that effect. If that were the point, then punishment of repentant wrongdoers would, indeed, be pointless. And if pointless, wrong. The point of society forcefully expressing its condemnation of what the wrongdoer did is to uphold its moral code by forcefully *declaring to one and all* that what he did was wrong. The wrongdoer's repentance does not undermine the social relevance of that declaration. Sometimes it's important for society to make that declaration even if the wrongdoer is repentant. In other cases, it's appropriate for society to forego making that declaration.

What are the implications for your work? I'm not sure. But this much I venture: those who say that ASJ should promote forgiveness by victims rather than seeking punishment of wrongdoers have a mistaken understanding of the proper role of forgiveness in our lives, or a mistaken understanding of the nature of punishment—or perhaps both. Forgiveness of a repentant wrongdoer for what he did to one is compatible with being in favor of society forcefully but justly expressing its condemnation of what he did by punishing him. Practicing forgiveness and seeking just punishment both have a place in the work of ASJ.

Your friend,
Nick

PART 3

JUSTICE, COALITIONS, AND KEEPING THE VISION ALIVE

16

The Importance of Forming
Networks and Coalitions

Dear Nick,

Thanks very much for that very helpful analysis of forgiveness and related concepts. I had not realized that, in my reflections on these matters, I had discerned a way of dealing with wrongdoing that is distinct both from forgiveness as understood in the philosophical/theological tradition and from forgiveness as understood in the therapeutic tradition. I see it all more clearly now.

Let me turn to an aspect of how ASJ works that hasn't yet come up in our discussion. Early in the history of ASJ we learned that collaborating with other organizations and communities is essential to our work. In your and my back-and-forth exchange up to this point it may have appeared that ASJ works alone. That is definitely not the case. In fact, one of the reasons our work has been effective is precisely because we have worked hard to form coalitions in which diverse voices unite around common goals such as reform in the police force or improvements in public education. So, in this letter, let me describe how we have worked to convene and organize diverse groups of people into coalitions in order to effect change.

Bringing groups with different interests and leadership together is not easy, but we have found it to be a very effective method of creating change. Some of ASJ's proudest achievements happened as the result of a joint effort. Many voices calling out together always draw more attention than a single, lone voice.

While we've worked with other organizations since we began this work, ASJ founded our first formal coalition of organizations in 2010 when we wanted to organize around reforms in public education and public health. To form the coalition Transformemos Honduras or "Let's Transform Honduras," we brought together health organizations; children's organizations like Compassion, World Vision, and Childfund; the German foreign aid agency; the development arm of the Catholic church; and the Church of God, one of Honduras' largest Protestant denominations.

People have asked us how we formed such formidable coalitions, and what the strategy is behind presenting some of our most public work through a shared platform. It was actually trickier than we had thought it would be, and we had to learn a lot about how to do it right; but ultimately we have experienced how effective a strong coalition can be.

When ASJ identifies a need for advocacy and intervention in Honduras, we begin by mapping and identifying organizations and the people within them that share common values in the area where we would like to work. We are interested in identifying people with both the interest and the connections to make change, which means we often begin with organizations that are already active on the issues that we care about.

We want to find people who share our goals, but also our hope. It's not very useful to have someone who staunchly opposes the status quo but scoffs at every proposal for change. There are many people who are overly cynical or negative about reform in Honduras. It's very difficult for those people to overcome their presuppositions and throw themselves behind the incremental changes we are working toward. We need people who not only have good ideas, but believe in them enough to take the risks needed to bring them about.

Once we have identified who would be helpful to have at our table, we call and invite them. This step quickly narrows the field of participants. Individuals or organizations that are not interested in joining forces will not show up to a meeting, or will come to an initial meeting but quickly stop attending. Our best allies are those who are willing to show up and keep showing up.

After we invited the first members to Transformemos Honduras (TH) and held our initial meetings, our work with the coalition was only beginning. As we would repeatedly find when we brought people together, we might have the best minds around the table, but in order to get anything done, we ourselves had to be willing to do the lion's share of the work.

That's the reality—everyone sitting on our coalition has a day job. Everyone is busy, so someone has to be willing to call everyone and find a time to meet that works with everyone's schedule, often upending his or her own schedule to make a time work; someone has to take minutes, do background research, write up studies, or arrange meetings. All this work is happening behind the scenes. It's difficult, frustrating work with little glory in it. But without ASJ's staff acting as the "motor" pushing everyone forward, a lot of the good ideas developed at those tables would have stalled.

This "motor" is particularly important when you realize how essential it is that the first few meetings of a coalition result in concrete plans leading to tangible change. Nothing is more frustrating than long, pointless meetings for meetings' sake. Coalitions should prioritize immediate, short-term goals that encourage participants and help them see that change is possible. We have found that there is a window of just a few months before people lose interest or enthusiasm and put their energy elsewhere. That is why, in our first meetings with TH, we were already making decisions, setting up meetings with authorities, and planning the studies we would be carrying out.

Maybe even more important than building a coalition is maintaining it. This is difficult because the people that make up a coalition aren't just representatives of their organization, they're individuals with their own time constraints, concerns, and needs. Our allies have sometimes gotten frustrated with ASJ and felt that we were not recognizing their contributions. Sometimes they were right! In our effort to get things done efficiently, we didn't always take time to appreciate and acknowledge everyone's roles. We have since tried to get better at making sure that the members of our coalitions are heard, their input considered, and their contributions recognized.

Over the years we have learned the importance of nurturing personal relationships in order to keep coalitions strong. I can't even count how many times one of us has invited an ally over for dinner, shown up at their office with their favorite coffee just to visit, or stopped by their homes to share encouraging words. On other occasions, we will act as a mediator between two allies that don't quite see eye to eye.

Nurturing the relationships that make up our coalitions is difficult and time-consuming work. It's not easy to balance ten or fifteen very different sets of needs and expectations. Some participants bring a level of celebrity that draws media and public attention to your cause, but also makes their schedules impossible. Other participants come with years of experience or training in an area and feel the need to speak at length at every meeting. As we balance the goals of the coalition with the individual needs of its members, it is particularly important to bring in people who are qualified, committed, but also understanding and forgiving when we aren't able to accommodate them as they would like.

Another important element when building a coalition is that members be willing to keep disagreements behind closed doors. I'm disappointed to say that some of our strongest critics over the years have been other nonprofit and justice organizations that were ostensibly on the same side as we were. Small disagreements about strategy can grow until they derail potential collaboration. One civil society leader served for a few years in one of our alliances while also participating actively in a different coalition that followed a different strategy. This person would sit with us as we prepared a statement, and then go out the next day and publicly contradict it. While we value a diversity of voices in our coalitions, we couldn't put up with someone publicly undermining our work. We work hard to make sure everyone in our coalitions feels heard and included, but we are also willing to ask people to leave when it's clear that their inclinations lie elsewhere.

Conflict and division can arise any time you bring together a group of people with different skills, opinions, and political views. They can slow efforts down or stop them completely. So why are we so committed to this model? Because we have found that operating in a coalition gives us credibility, protection, diversity of expertise, and allows us to expand our work beyond what our staff can do alone.

We think the benefits of being part of these coalitions far outweigh the costs.

First of all, there is credibility in allies with more experience. When we first founded the Alliance for Peace and Justice (APJ), which I mentioned in a previous letter, and called a press conference with Julieta Castellanos, who was director of Honduras' National University, or Alberto Solórzano, who was the director of the entire evangelical association, media sources paid attention. Castellanos and Solórzano could get appointments that we could not, and their presence on our coalitions brought us quickly before government ministers, and even the president. Once we were in those meetings, our advocacy points had to stand on their own merits—but many worthwhile causes are shut down before they begin because they cannot even get a seat at the table. Having the right allies helps us with that.

Second, acting as a coalition offers protection to the coalition's members, particularly when you are saying something difficult or unpopular. In December 2016, one of our board members, Jorge Machado, was targeted in an assassination attempt for his work on the police reform commission. Immediately, our allies came together and presented a united front demanding investigation into the case and stating unequivocal support for the police reform process. Showing a united front with other well-known figures helps to protect us and shows that we won't be taken down easily. Political leaders might be willing to attack a single anti-corruption organization, but probably not a leader of the Protestant church who has overseen the pastors for almost half the country.

Another benefit to working in coalitions is that it expands our strengths and abilities. We have allies, for example, who are excellent at political analysis. They have access to information that we do not, and are very good at analyzing what is going on in the complicated world of Honduran politics. We are not experts in everything, and by strategically seeking out allies we have been able to expand our understanding and to operate in a more informed way.

Coalitions also help give us a wider reach. I think we at ASJ have a tendency to want to do everything, and diversifying our voices has allowed us to not spread ourselves too thin. The goal is never that ASJ be responsible for every justice initiative in Honduras. Now, instead of expanding our youth programs to new neighborhoods, we are helping other churches and organizations open similar programs in their own communities. Instead of investigating more individual cases of homicide, we are accompanying the National Police force to investigate more cases using our methodology. Letting go of control can be difficult, but when we identify capable and committed allies, we can see the impact of our work spread far beyond what our staff could do alone.

As I have said repeatedly, building and maintaining coalitions is not easy. But the final and I think most convincing reason we have seen to operate in coalitions is the impact that we can create when we join forces with organizations across the political spectrum, Protestant and Catholic, Christian and secular. In Honduras, for example, we are seeing dramatic change in the National Police force with more than a third of the corrupt force fired and strict new controls put in place. These are country-transforming statistics. You can also see transformation in the number of days of class in public schools, in the decreasing number of "ghost" public employees, in the way public contracting is managed. These changes are a result of diverse public figures and civil society leaders convening around similar ideas and speaking out with a common voice. Journalists would come to us to get an interview, they would go to World Vision, they would go to the National University, they would go to church leaders, and they would hear the same ideas repeated over and over again—purge the police, reform public education, hold those in power accountable.

This is what makes our work in coalitions worth it—being part of a broad network of voices sharing the same message of peace and justice for Honduras.

Your friend,
Kurt

17

Justice Is Grounded in Rights

Dear Kurt,

Thanks for that very illuminating description of some of the networks and coalitions that ASJ has formed over the years, and for your explanation of why you in ASJ regard it as important to establish these connections and not "go it alone."

In my first letter to you I noted that, when I first went down to Honduras to observe what ASJ was doing, I was at once struck by the fact that ASJ is, very intentionally, a *justice* organization—not a relief or development organization, but a justice organization. I remarked that I might have inferred that from the name of the organization, Association for a More Just Society. But over the years I have learned that the name of an organization often does not tell us much about what the organization actually does.

But justice comes in a number of different forms. So in previous letters I distinguished between what I called *first-order* justice and *second-order* justice, and I identified some of the diverse forms that second-order corrective justice can take—restorative justice versus punitive justice being a major distinction. I also highlighted an important distinction within punitive justice: punishment as retribution versus punishment as reproval. I hope, Kurt, that my drawing these distinctions has proved illuminating rather than dizzying!

While some of the work of ASJ is in the area of second-order corrective justice, most of it is now in the area of first-order social justice.

I explained first-order justice as justice in our ordinary interactions with each other—teachers and students treating each other

95

justly, parents and children treating each other justly, merchants and clients treating each other justly, etc. But I did not explain what is it to treat another person justly. It's time for me now to do that. My aim, in what follows, is not to present an abstract disquisition on justice but to illuminate what ASJ does.

There are, as one would expect, different answers to the question, what is it to treat someone justly—or unjustly. Let me present my own answer without doing much here to defend that answer against alternative answers. (I have defended my answer against alternative answers, and developed my answer more fully than I do here, in my book *Justice: Rights and Wrongs*.)

Coming down to us from antiquity are two, fundamentally different, ways of thinking of justice in general. One of these was first formulated by the ancient Greek philosopher Aristotle (384–322 BCE). Justice, said Aristotle, consists of equity in the distribution of benefits and burdens. The other way of thinking of justice was first formulated by the ancient Roman jurist Ulpian (170–223 CE). Justice, said Ulpian, consists of rendering to each person his or her *due* or *right*. (Ulpian's Latin word that I have translated as "due" or "right" is *jus*.)

I much prefer the Ulpian formula. There are, of course, many cases of injustice for which the Aristotelian formula captures why they are cases of injustice: some benefit or burden has been distributed inequitably. But there are also many cases of injustice for which the Aristotelian formula fails us. Of the many examples I could mention, let me confine myself to just one. Suppose that, unbeknownst to you, I invade your privacy in some way; I read some of your private correspondence, gain access to your email, whatever. In such a case, I have not treated you in a way that is due you, in a way that you have a right to be treated; I have violated the Ulpian formula for justice. But there has been no inequitable distribution of benefits and burdens.

What now requires explanation is, what it is to have a *right* to being treated a certain way—what it is for a certain way of being treated to be *due* one.

The first thing to say here is that if one has a right to being treated a certain way, then being treated that way would be a *good* thing in one's life, never a bad thing. I don't have a right to someone breaking my leg—unless, perchance, I'm in a car accident and the only way to extricate me from the wreckage is to break my leg.

But though a right is always a way of being treated that would be a good thing in one's life, there are many ways of being treated that would be a good thing in one's life to which one does not have a right. In some of my writings I have offered a somewhat whimsical example to make the point. I think it would be a great good in my life were the Rijksmuseum in Amsterdam to offer me Rembrandt's great painting, *The Jewish Bride*, to hang on my living room wall, along with a security force to stand guard. But though that would be a great good in my life, I don't have a right to it. The Rijksmuseum is not wronging me, not depriving me of what I have a right to, by not giving me that painting. Their not doing so is not an infraction of justice.

Why not? Why do we have a right to some good ways of being treated and not to other good ways of being treated? What accounts for the difference? As one would expect, there is also no consensus on how this question should be answered. Let me, once again, present my own answer without defending it against alternative answers.

To answer the question as I think it should be answered, we have to bring two fundamental facts about human beings into the picture. One is the fact that every human being has worth or excellence in certain respects; every human being is praiseworthy in certain respects. That is to say: not only are the *lives* of human beings better and worse in certain respects; human beings are *themselves* better and worse in certain respects, more worthy of praise and less worthy of praise. We each have moral worth in certain respects and to certain degrees; we each have worth on account of our accomplishments; and we each have the ineradicable worth of being a recipient of the love that God bestows on all creatures who bear God's image.

The other fact about human beings that we have to bring into the picture is that we can treat others in ways that befit their worth and in ways that do not befit their worth. If you are a student in a course I am teaching and you have done top-notch work, then what befits the academic worth you have thereby acquired is that, in the American system, I give you an A for the course. Anything less than that would not befit the worth you have acquired.

Using these two ideas, I can now explain how I understand rights. You have a right to the good of my treating you a certain way just in case, if I did not treat you that way, I would not be treating you as befits your worth—not treating you with due respect for your worth, instead belittling you, treating you with disrespect. Rights are what respect for worth requires. If you have done top-notch work in my course, then you have a right to the good of my giving you an A because, if I gave you anything less than that, I would not be treating you as befits your academic worth.

Consider any example of social injustice that ASJ has brought to light: injustice in the educational system, injustice in the system for the distribution of medicines, injustice in the police force. I submit that, in each case, if one looks closely, one will find that the rights—natural or legal—of certain members of Honduran society were being violated. Take an example that you have mentioned several times in your letters. The laws of Honduras give every child the legal right to at least 200 days of class per year; ASJ discovered that many were receiving no more than 125 days. They were being deprived of what they have a right to. They were being treated in a way that does not befit the worth they have as young full-fledged members of Honduran society in need of education. They were being treated as pawns in a corrupt system. They were being treated with indignity.

The work of ASJ consists, at bottom, of bringing to light the various ways in which the laws, regulations, and social practices of Honduras violate people's rights, the various ways in which they do not treat the members of Honduran society as befits their multi-faceted worth—and then, that done, of trying to change those laws, regulations, and social practices so that people are treated with due respect for their worth. Respect for the worth, the dignity, of each and every member of Honduran society is the deep motivation of everything ASJ does.

In concluding this letter, let me note that, given the understanding of justice and rights that I have just now presented, we can now understand, at a deeper level, a point that I made very briefly in my first letter, namely, that working for justice is typically dangerous whereas merely working to improve people's lives is typically not dangerous.

Here's why. The person who works for justice identifies *victims of injustice*. To identify someone as a victim of injustice is to declare that they have been *wronged*, deprived of what they have a right to. Wronged *by someone*, of course. To seek justice for that wronged person requires that one identify those who are wronging them, declare that they are wrongdoers, and insist that they cease and desist. Seeking justice is, in that way, inherently a moral engagement of a certain sort—a moral engagement of an unpleasant sort, one that most of us would prefer to avoid. It requires making a moral accusation. The accusation may be expressed in gentle terms; it need not be harsh. But moral accusation is inherent to the attempt to undo injustice.

No one likes being the brunt of a moral accusation. It stirs up anger, hostility, resentment. Those who are responsible for perpetrating social injustice typically profit, in one way or another, from what they are doing. For them to acknowledge this fact would require that they give up their position of privilege and power. And that, they don't want to do. It is my impression, however, that in many cases, perhaps most, what provokes the hostility of those accused of wrongdoing is not just the prospect of their privilege and power going down the drain, but resentment at being the brunt of moral accusation.

Your friend,
Nick

18

When Rights Are Violated

Dear Nick,

Thanks for your description of "rights" as the basis for understanding justice. You've given me language to think about many of the instances of injustice we witness daily here in Honduras. Because these sorts of discussions can often feel theoretical or abstract, I want to give some examples of how the violation of rights can affect people that I've met personally. It often helps me to ground these broader ideas in some individual names and stories.

For example, ASJ did a study a few years ago about private security companies in Honduras that are contracted to protect government institutions like public universities and hospitals. Honduran law sets the minimum wage for the employees of these sorts of companies at about $450 per month. The law also lays out benefits including overtime, health care, and vacation and sick days. Security companies that abide by these legal minimums aren't doing their employees any favors, they're simply providing them with their due. So when we found that the majority of security guards were paid far less than the minimum wage with next to no benefits, even after working exhausting twenty-four-hour shifts, we knew this was a clear case of injustice.

One guard we spoke with, Abigail, told us how uniforms and supplies were deducted from her meager paycheck, which was one-third less than it should have been by law. During her twelve-hour shifts, she was prohibited from sitting or resting and was forced to eat her meals quickly in the same cramped closet where the guards kept their things.

Abigail was wronged by her employers, and wronged by the state institution that hired a company without doing its due diligence to ensure that the employees would be treated well. She is just one of more than 75,000 private security guards in the country who are also being wronged. These guards each have their own hopes and dreams. Abigail told us she wanted to become a nurse. Others may hope to start a small business, or travel to another country, or become a famous soccer player. ASJ can't do much to help these individuals reach their dreams, even if doing so would be, as you say, "a great good" in their lives. But we certainly can, and should, work to grant them access to what is due them as their right. We are working with the Ministry of Security and the Ministry of Labor to increase accountability over private security companies so that guards across the country will someday soon receive the minimum wage and benefits to which they are entitled by law.

I can think of so many stories of people whose rights are similarly ignored. Sonia, a woman from my church, is a nurse, but cannot find work despite her professional degree. This is because public hospitals in Honduras tend to only hire staff belonging to whatever political party is in power. Sonia belongs to the wrong political party, and so is denied access to the opportunities that would improve her family's situation.

Another example: the Honduran constitution states that access to water is a human right; but while water is piped into wealthy communities every other day, our community's taps work only once per month. Too often, our neighbors have to spend money they don't have to buy water from trucks just to have enough to drink and to cook with.

The common thread of all these stories of injustice is that Abigail, Sonia, and the people of Nueva Suyapa aren't just lacking things that they would like to have, things that would be "great goods" in their lives. Instead, something is being taken from them that they are owed, to which they have a right—the salary they worked for, a job interview without discrimination, clean water that the government has already promised to provide. Thinking of their concerns in this way focuses attention not on their need, but on the companies and government agencies that are failing to meet that need.

As I look back at my examples, it all seems so clear-cut. The work of justice includes ensuring that everyone has that to which they have a right. You have done much more writing and speaking on this topic: has anyone pushed back on this?

Your friend,
Kurt

19

In Defense of Talk about Rights

Dear Kurt,

I have had pushback. Some writers who agree with me that justice is grounded in rights prefer a different account of rights from my dignity-based account; others dislike the very idea of rights and try to explain justice without appealing to rights. In this letter, let me address the objections of those who oppose rights-talk.

When I have given public talks in which I argued that justice is grounded in rights, I have almost invariably gotten a pushback in the question period afterwards from some members of the audience who insisted that we should not be talking about rights but instead about love or responsibility. I vividly remember a friend of mine standing up after one of my talks and saying, with great intensity, "Nick, nobody has any rights. It's grace all the way down."

What problem do people have with rights-talk? Different people have different problems, naturally. I have a friend whose experience is that an appeal to rights typically shuts off further discussion. Imagine a public forum in which the topic of discussion is whether the city can afford to install heating in some of the downtown sidewalks to melt the snow and ice in the winter and thus make the walks safer (not a topic of discussion in Honduras!). The discussion goes back and forth until someone in favor of heated sidewalks ups the ante by declaring that citizens have a *right* to safe, ice-free sidewalks. Now the rest of us can no longer discuss whether the city can *afford* to install heating in some of the downtown sidewalks; we have to deal with the much more arcane issue of whether citizens have a *right* to heated sidewalks. The discussion falters; there's little more to do than take a vote.

This way of using rights-talk reflects a feature of rights that I have not, up to this point, called attention to. Philosophers call it the *trumping force* of rights (sometimes they call it, instead, the *peremptory force* of rights). The idea is that if you have a right to being treated a certain way by me, then, no matter how many good things I can bring about by *not* treating you that way, I ought to treat you that way. Your right to being treated that way trumps all those goods. Suppose, for example, that you are a student in one of my courses who has turned in a top-notch essay, for which you deserve an A (in the American system of grading). But I find you to be rather cocky and full of yourself, and I judge that a B-minus, accompanied by some marginal notes in which I make the B-minus seem plausible by highlighting flaws in your work, might well induce some desirable character reformation. So I give you a B-minus. (I once had a colleague who told me that he had done exactly this!) No matter. You have a right to an A, so I ought to give you an A. Period! Your right to an A trumps the goods that a B-minus might bring about. If I think your character needs reforming, I will have to think of some other way of inducing that.

I have another friend who has spent his career working in international health organizations and is opposed to rights-talk because, in his experience, an appeal to rights was all too often used by those who favored some project to make those who were opposed feel guilty for being opposed. He recalls a discussion about whether or not the reduction of river blindness in Africa should be given priority over other health concerns. After the issue had been discussed for some time, one of the participants stood up and declared that people in Africa have a *right* to the elimination of river blindness—the suggestion being, "how could anybody of good character possibly be opposed to giving it priority," this at a time when no one knew how to eliminate river blindness!

My response to these two friends is that, common though these ways of using rights-talk may be, they are an *abuse* of rights-talk. It's an abuse of rights-talk to use it to close down discussion, it's an abuse of rights-talk to use it to make one's opponents feel guilty. Faced with such abuse, what we should do is oppose the abuse, not reject all rights-talk because it is sometimes abused. Every component of our moral vocabulary is susceptible to abuse—talk of love is susceptible to abuse, talk of obligation is. If the abuse of some component in our moral vocabulary were a good reason for no longer using that component, we would have no moral vocabulary left.

A number of philosophers and theologians have mounted a quite different line of objection to the use of rights-talk. They point to a malignant component of modern Western culture that they call *possessive individualism*, and they argue that rights-talk functions to express this malign attitude. The possessive individualist, rather than taking note of his responsibilities, talks only about his rights.

A good many of those who lodge this objection to rights-talk think to bolster their case by appealing to a widely believed narrative concerning the origin of the idea of *natural* rights (in distinction from legal rights). According to the narrative, the idea of natural rights was devised by the individualist philosophers of the secular European Enlightenment, and it continues to bear the telltale signs of its origins.

In some of my writings I have discussed, in considerable detail, this line of objection to the use of rights-talk (especially in *Justice: Rights and Wrongs*); here let me briefly make just two points in response. First, it has decisively been shown that the narrative is false. The groundbreaking book in this regard was Brian Tierney's *The Idea of Natural Rights* (1997). Tierney, a specialist in the history of medieval legal thought, showed that the canon lawyers of the twelfth century were explicitly using the idea of natural rights. It turns out that the idea of natural rights emerged from the cradle of medieval Christendom, not from the individualist philosophers of the Enlightenment.

Second, reflect on the fact that a right is to the good of being treated a certain way by someone. It takes two or more to have a right. Rights are social relationships—*normative* social relationships. A right is not something one has all by oneself—as a solitary individual. (An exception would be, one's rights to how one treats oneself—if there are such rights!) And just as I have rights with respect to how you treat me, so also you have rights with respect to how I treat you. Rights are, in that way, symmetrical.

What follows is that the person who speaks only about *his* right to being treated certain ways *by others*, and never acknowledges the rights of *others* to be treated certain ways *by him*, is abusing the language of rights. There are, indeed, possessive individualists in our society, and their use of rights-talk is indeed one of the ways in which they express their possessive individualism. But the culprit in the situation is not the language of rights but the mentality of possessive individualism, a mentality that wrests the language of rights to its own malign purposes.

Consider the counterpart situation for persons of an authoritarian bent and their employment of obligation-talk. Such persons never hesitate to point to the obligations others have toward them, while ignoring the obligations they have toward others. This is an abuse of obligation-talk. The culprit in the situation is not the language of obligation but the authoritarian personality that finds the language of obligations useful for its malign purposes.

What does one do when confronted with someone who is abusing rights-talk? One calls them out for the abuse. One reminds the person who declares that we all have a right to heated sidewalks that the discussion is whether the city can afford to install heated sidewalks; if the city cannot afford it, then nobody has a right to it. One calls to the attention of the person who declares that people in Africa have a right to the elimination of river blindness that we don't know how to eliminate river blindness; if we don't know how to eliminate river blindness, then nobody has a right to its elimination. The general principle is this: if it is impossible for me to treat you a certain way, or if I cannot afford to, or if I don't know how, then you don't have a right to being treated that way. And as for the possessive individualist: one forcefully calls to his attention that just as he has a right to be treated in certain ways by others, others have a right to be treated in certain ways by him.

My remarks thus far in this letter have been defensive in character: I have argued that several of the objections commonly made against rights-talk turn out not to be objections to the use of rights-talk as such but objections to one or another abuse of rights-talk. Let me now step out of this defensive stance and ask: what would be lost if, for some reason, we could no longer speak of rights? What would be lost if ASJ could no longer speak of the rights of those whom it stands alongside of? Those who advocate the abolition of rights-talk seldom if ever ask what would be lost if we did in fact abolish rights-talk from our moral vocabulary. Let me point to two things of great importance that would be lost.

First, we would no longer have available to us what I called, earlier in this letter, the *trumping* function of rights. The example I gave to make the point was rather trivial: if you have written a top-notch essay in a course I am teaching, then you have a right to an A; and your having that rights implies that, no matter how many goods I might bring about by giving you a B-minus, I *ought* to give you an A. Period!

Far more weighty examples are ready at hand. The twentieth century was full of political regimes that believed it was acceptable to treat some human beings as disposable if doing so would bring about some great good for others. If we cannot appeal to the rights of human beings, if we cannot argue that to treat human beings in such a way is a violation of how they have a right to be treated, and hence is off the table, we have no language for denouncing this manipulative, utilitarian, "calculus of goods" way of thinking.

Recall my description, in my second letter, of my experience in South Africa in 1975. Let us grant, purely for the sake of the argument, that the segregated society the Afrikaners envisioned, in which each nationality would discover and live out its own cultural identity, would have been a good thing. The massive violation of rights perpetrated on the people of color meant that achieving that ideal by apartheid was wrong, impermissible. The Afrikaners took no note of the rights of people of color, only of their own (self-perceived) benevolence. Their failure to take note of the rights of people of color meant that there was no brake on their paternalistic benevolence.

Now for a second thing of great importance that would be lost if we no longer had available to us the language of rights and its corollaries. Recall that that to which one has a right is always the good of being treated a certain way by someone. And then take note of the use of the passive voice in this formula: *being treated* a certain way.

I submit that the moral order has two fundamental dimensions: the agent-dimension and the patient-dimension, the actor-dimension and the recipient-dimension. On the one hand, there is the moral significance of what we do; on the other hand, there is the moral significance of how we are done unto. On the one hand, there is the moral significance of how we treat others; on the other hand, there is the moral significance of how we are treated by others. In thinking about the moral order, the Western philosophical tradition has focused almost all of its attention on the agent-dimension. In doing so it has, in my judgment, presented a seriously incomplete and distorted picture of the moral order as a whole.

The language of duty and obligation, and its companion language of being guilty, is for bringing to speech (one aspect of) the agent-dimension of the moral order. By contrast, the language of rights, and its companion language of being wronged, is for bringing to speech the recipient-dimension of the moral order—the dimension of how we are done unto.

Consider an abused wife, and suppose that the only language available to her is the agent-language of duty, obligation, guilt, and so forth. With such language, she can call attention to the moral condition of her abusive husband: he is guilty of failing to treat her as he ought to treat her, as he has a duty and a responsibility to treat her, guilty of failing to act lovingly, and so forth. What she cannot do is call attention to *her own* moral condition, namely, that she has been *wronged*, not treated in a way that befits her worth, treated with disrespect, demeaned. Rights-talk and its corollaries enable her to call attention to *her* moral condition. I submit that it would be a great loss if she did not have available to her the language for calling attention to the moral significance of how she has been done unto, namely, that she has been wronged, demeaned, treated with disrespect.

What these reflections show is that there's a reason why ASJ often uses the language of rights in speaking of what it does. The fundamental strategy of ASJ is to stand up with and for those whom it identifies as victims of injustice in Honduran society, and then to defend their cause by trying to get government officials to do what they ought to be doing. ASJ does not start from the moral condition of officials, namely, that they are guilty of not doing what they ought to be doing. It starts from the moral condition of the victims: their rights are being violated. It starts from the wronged, not from the guilty.

Imagine how different the work of ASJ would be if no language were available for calling attention to the moral condition of the wronged. It could call attention to the moral condition of government officials, namely, that they are guilty of failing to carry out their duties. But it could not call attention to the moral condition of the victims, namely, that they are *wronged*. It could call attention to the pitiable condition of the victims; but *pitiable* is not a moral category. The reason rights-language has been the preferred language for social protest movements in the twentieth century—witness the movement for labor rights, for women's rights, for children's rights, for civil rights—is that such language enables the oppressed and their supporters to call attention to their moral condition.

Your friend,
Nick

20

Justice Work Makes People Mad

Dear Nick,

Your letter has certainly given me a lot to think about. I appreciate your highlighting of the way "rights-talk" can be abused. While I feel that an understanding of human rights is essential, at ASJ we have been stymied in the past by what you point to—that once rights-talk gets "trotted out," it becomes very difficult to return to a discussion about what is feasible or affordable. If someone has a right to a quality education, the argument goes, no reform short of total transformation of the educational system should be accepted.

There have been many occasions where we have gone to a government authority to challenge them for something we see as injustice, whether that is corruption in a government contract, or the fact that millions of Hondurans still do not have adequate access to medicine in public hospitals. We may come with ten recommendations for improvement, and ultimately, we may only achieve four of those recommendations. In those situations, our team still celebrates. This, of course, does not mean that our work is over or that we should be satisfied with that limited reform. But the fact that we haven't seen a complete transformation in the government institution doesn't negate the progress we have seen.

I also appreciated the clarity of your distinction between, as you say, "the moral significance of what we do" and "the moral significance of how we are done unto." You are right that this language is important to the work of ASJ. We are not simply moralizing, telling government officials that they must act better—we are working systemically, seeking to change the systems that allow such actions to harm and oppress the Honduran population.

This distinction pushes us to focus not on a few examples of injustice, but on the core issues that most affect the poorest Hondurans. Other organizations make different decisions. Rather than focus on the issues that affect the majority of people in a country, an organization might choose to work on issues that most seriously affect a specific group—such as people who have been enslaved or trafficked, people with rare diseases, or people who are starving.

I can understand the motivations behind that type of work. Sex trafficking, for example, is a justice issue that feels so black and white that it seems easy to get people on board. Some organizations seem to hope that if they can mobilize people around a really black and white issue, or if they can get the justice system to work in the most egregious cases, then this can generate momentum to create change in other areas, or prompt the system to work better overall. However, I am not sure that this strategy achieves its goal.

What I have seen is the reverse: efforts to change a specific thematic area tend to help only for as long as financial or technical support in that area continues. If efforts aren't also made to change the underlying government systems, then as soon as support ends, positive reforms falter or get worse.

We believe that long-term, systems-strengthening work is the best way to work for justice, both first-order and second-order; but we also know that it's more complicated, difficult, and dangerous.

Projects like food pantries, water projects, or toys for needy children seem so obviously good that anyone criticizing them must be some sort of cynical Grinch. But while work in these areas can do real good for some people, none of them are necessarily doing the hard work of addressing root causes, asking why people are poor, or hungry, or why they don't have access to water. These projects also don't pass my litmus test for justice work—they don't make anyone mad.

In fact, these projects may actually reinforce existing unjust structures. Corrupt government officials in Kenya are happy that foreign groups come in to dig wells—it allows them to continue to pocket money earmarked for local infrastructure. Companies that pay less than a living wage in the United States are happy that a food pantry provides employees' needs unmet by their insufficient salaries.

Justice work is different. Justice work makes people mad. It's a point you have made several times in these letters. Let me give the point specificity by spelling out in more detail how ASJ works and why it takes on the projects that it does.

When Dionisio Díaz García stood up for the thousands of security guards and cleaning employees in Honduras who were not receiving the minimum wage, the company hired assassins to kill him. When ASJ's board members joined a commission to clean up Honduras' corrupt police force, they were targeted with constant harassment and death threats; one survived a murder attempt that killed his bodyguard.

When you go after the teachers who are taking a salary without showing up to work, they get mad. When you go after Congressional representatives who charge personal luxuries to government funds, they get mad. When you uncover a sex trafficking network, the people running it get mad, and so do the government officials bribed to look the other way.

We want the police, the legal system, and the courts in Honduras to work not only in these worst cases, but in any case that they take on. We want justice for the victims of trafficking, but we also want justice for the woman mopping floors for barely half of the legal minimum wage, for the teenage girl coerced into a "relationship" with a gang member, or for the woman murdered by a jealous husband.

At ASJ, we work in only one country, and we work on the issues we have found make the most impact on the greatest number of people in the country—corruption and violence. One huge benefit of this narrow focus is that in many of our priority issues we are working with the same players, the same public perception, the same resources, and, of course, the same culture, context, and history. This allows us to build up a reputation and purvey our success in one area into initiatives in other areas.

A few years ago, for example, we offered technical assistance throughout the selection process of a new team of anti-corruption judges, officials charged with prosecuting cases of corruption in the

Honduran courts. Our collaboration with the judiciary and the international anti-corruption body MACCIH helped ensure that the hiring process was merit-based rather than politicized. With every corruption conviction, we see the results of this effort, and the experience has opened new doors.

Two months later we were asked to help select prosecutors for a new anti-corruption unit in the Attorney General's office. When that process went well, we were invited to help design the selection process for every judge in the country! Each subsequent step was informed by our past experience in this country, and by our two decades of building up experience, developing relationships, and establishing a reputation as technical leaders in anti-corruption.

ASJ is currently involved with overseeing or supporting dozens of different projects—from the hiring of doctors, to revamping the national registry of people, and to other projects we had never planned or dreamed about.

When I visit conferences or speak to colleges and find students passionate about providing access to water, or ending human trafficking, I'm glad that they've found an issue that they care about. However, I also encourage them to ask more questions, to analyze the root causes of the issue and the structures that allow it to perpetuate. If they feel called to this work, I challenge them to think deeply rather than broadly, to find a single location to work in and to commit to it for long enough to understand its unique dynamics. When people think about injustice, they often imagine serving in far-off places; it can be a surprise to them to learn that there are also significant justice issues in their own hometown.

Justice work isn't just something happening "elsewhere." The US experiences deep inequalities in its education system and health care system. For example, poor school districts invest 15 percent less in their students than nearby districts that are not poor. Four US cities—St. Louis, Baltimore, New Orleans, and Detroit—are among the fifty most violent cities in the world, while not a single European or Asian city makes the list.

When such issues are in our own backyard, we recognize their complexity. We don't assume we can jump in and make a big difference right away. We're afraid of political backlash, we know that there are many different ideas of what might work. Everyone in the US might think it's great that you're going to visit the Ukraine to work on corruption, but start talking about corruption in US politics and some of your friends may become enemies.

Doing justice around the world is a good and admirable thing; but anyone can do justice wherever they are. The question isn't how far but how deep you are willing to go.

Your friend,
Kurt

21

Beyond Justice: Shalom

Dear Kurt,

In my attempt to articulate the perspective that I discern behind the work of ASJ, I have thus far maintained a rather sharp focus on justice, both first-order and second-order, and on ancillary phenomena such as rights, dignity, etc. In this letter, I want to take a wider view.

The Old Testament/Hebrew Bible book of Jeremiah reports the prophet Jeremiah as saying to his fellow Jewish exiles in Babylon, "Seek the shalom of the city, for in its shalom you will find your shalom" (29:7). Assuming that there is both individual shalom and communal shalom, the prophet declares that the former requires the latter. No doubt he also thought that the latter requires the former: if the community is to enjoy shalom, its members must enjoy shalom. In this letter, I want to set ASJ's justice work within the broader context of seeking shalom.

The Hebrew word *shalom* occurs dozens of times, perhaps even hundreds of times, in the Hebrew text of the Old Testament/Hebrew Bible. It has usually been translated into English as "peace." I regard that as a very poor translation. Shalom does indeed require that the members of the community live at peace with each other and that the community as a whole be at peace with its neighbors. But, as we shall see, shalom goes beyond peace, beyond the absence of hostility.

The New Revised Standard Version translates "shalom" in Jeremiah 29:7 as "welfare." I judge that to be better than "peace." But in present-day English, "welfare" has economistic connotations; we speak of the "welfare state." "Shalom" has no such connotations.

I think the best translation of "shalom" into present-day English is "flourishing." "Seek the flourishing of the city," says the prophet to his fellow Jews in exile, "for in its flourishing you will find your flourishing."

There are, as one would expect, different ways of understanding what it is for a community and its members to flourish. No biblical writer defines the term *shalom*. But when we look at the passages in which the term occurs in the biblical writings and interpret those passages in context, what comes through is a clear picture of the sort of flourishing that the biblical writers had in mind when they spoke of shalom. Shalom consists of flourishing in all dimensions of our existence: in our relations to our fellow human beings, in our relations to the physical world, in our relation to God, in our relations to the artifacts and institutions created by human beings, even in our relation to ourselves.

Perhaps the most prominent theme in what the biblical writers say about shalom is their insistence on the inextricable connection between shalom and justice. Justice is a necessary condition of shalom; without justice, there is no shalom. To cite just one of many passages, the prophet Isaiah declares that when "justice dwells in the wilderness and doing right abides in the fruitful field, the effect . . . will be shalom" (Isa 32:16). I should note, Kurt, that I have replaced "righteousness" in the NRSV with "doing right." I think "doing right" better captures the thought. Righteousness is a character trait. I think it makes no sense to say that a certain character trait "abides in the fruitful field." Even if those who are treated unjustly have resigned themselves to their lot, even if they live at peace with their oppressors, shalom is absent. Shalom would have been absent in the United States before emancipation *even if* the slaves had been content with their lot—which most of them were not, though the slaveholders typically said they were. Shalom is a moral condition.

Shalom in our social relationships goes beyond justice, however. Shalom is present in our social relationships when we are not only related to each other in ways that are good for us and just, but when we find joy and satisfaction in being so related. Shalom is not only a moral condition but also an experiential condition.

Another component of shalom is flourishing in our relation to the physical world. Shalom is present insofar as we, bodily creatures and not disembodied souls, are related to the earth and its creatures in ways that are good for us and right, and we find joy and satisfaction in being so related to the physical world, including our bodies. In speaking of shalom, Isaiah foresees a day when the Lord will prepare

> a banquet of rich fare for all the people,
> a banquet of wines well matured and richest fare,
> well matured wines strained clear (Isa 25:6).

A third component of shalom, for the biblical writers the most fundamental component, is flourishing in our relation to God. When the prophets speak of shalom, they foresee a day when human beings flourish in the love and service of God. In the words, once more, of the prophet Isaiah:

> The mountain of the house of the LORD
> shall be established as the highest of the mountains,
> and shall be raised above the hills;
> all the nations shall flow to it,
> and many peoples shall come and say:
> "Come, let us go up to the mountain of the LORD,
> to the house of the God of Jacob,
> that the LORD may teach us the ways of the LORD
> and that we may walk in the paths of the LORD."   (Isa 2:2–3)

Shalom is present insofar as we are related to God in ways that are good for us and right, and we find joy and satisfaction in being so related to God.

I am not aware that the biblical writers ever speak of shalom in connection with our relation to ourselves, or in connection with our relation to human artifacts and institutions. But from what they say about shalom in our relationships to each other, to the physical world, and to God, surely we can extrapolate to these additional relationships.

Back now to where I began. I think it is illuminating to see the work of ASJ in Honduran society within the larger context of seeking the shalom of Honduran society and its members. The sharply focused justice work of ASJ is an important component within the larger project of seeking the shalom of the city and its inhabitants. It helps to keep that larger project in mind.

You may have noticed that each time I spoke of shalom in our relationships, I emphasized that shalom includes being related in ways that are *good for us and right (or just)*—being related to one's fellows, to the physical world, to God, in ways that are good for us and right (or just). Shalom also includes finding joy and satisfaction in those relationships; but being related in ways that are good for us and right (or just) is necessary.

In my exposition of the shalom understanding of flourishing, I have appealed to various writings in the Hebrew Bible/Old Testament. But I don't want to give the impression that this understanding of flourishing is just "Old Testament stuff." Quite to the contrary, as I am sure you know, it is carried forward into the New Testament. The Greek work translated as "peace" in our standard New Testament translations is *eirenē*. In the ancient Septuagint translation of the Hebrew Bible into Greek, this was the word used to translate the Hebrew *shalom*. Jesus, in his farewell discourse to his disciples, says, "Peace (shalom), I leave with you, my peace (shalom) I give to you" (John 14:27). His first words to his disciples after his resurrection were, "Peace (shalom) be with you" (John 20:21). His prophetic messianic title was "Prince of Peace (shalom)" (Isa 9:6). The point could be developed at length.

The understanding of flourishing that guides most social science research today, and has guided it for many years, namely, the utilitarian understanding, is different on this point. The utilitarian starts from how people experience their lives, specifically, from the degree to which they find their lives overall satisfying or happy. His basic thesis is that the more satisfying a person finds his or her life overall, the more that person is flourishing.

It's easy to see why social scientists, and activists trained by social scientists, find this utilitarian understanding of flourishing attractive: the standard tools of social scientific research are adequate, or appear to be adequate, for determining the degree to which individuals are flourishing. On the assumption that individuals, though not infallible, are nonetheless rather good judges of how satisfying they find their lives, one asks them to rate their satisfaction. Thereby one supposedly gets a rather good indication of the degree to which they are flourishing.

The person who understands flourishing as shalom agrees with the utilitarian that satisfaction with how one's life is going is an indispensable component of shalom. The person who is depressed, even though her life, objectively observed, is going well, is not fully flourishing. The shalom theorist disagrees, however, with the assumption of the utilitarian that satisfaction is sufficient for flourishing. People find satisfaction in what is not good for them, excessive drinking, for example, and fail to find satisfaction in what is good for them, regular exercise, for example. So too, they find satisfaction in doing what is morally wrong, and fail to find satisfaction in doing what is morally right. And, as I noted earlier, sometimes those whose life-condition is unjust—slaves, for example—seem to accept their circumstances. The shalom theorist holds that, in all such cases, the person is not fully flourishing. A person is truly flourishing only if she is related to herself and her surroundings in ways that are morally right or just and objectively good for her.

An implication of this point is that the standard social science research methods are inadequate for fully determining shalom. One has to go beyond assessing subjective experiences of satisfaction and make objective, evaluative, and normative judgments. If I care about a friend's flourishing, I must be willing to say to him, should the occasion arise, that what he is doing or experiencing is not good for him, or is not right (or just), no matter how satisfying he may find it.

I admire ASJ very much for its sharp focus on justice; ASJ does not flail about! What I have tried to show in this letter is that, in seeking justice in Honduras, ASJ is thereby contributing to the flourishing—

the shalom—of Honduran society. It seems to me important to keep this more comprehensive picture in mind. Justice work can become grim and abstract. Yes, our aim is to bring it about that people enjoy their rights. But to enjoy one's rights is, so far forth, to flourish—to experience shalom.

Your friend,
Nick

22

The *Spirit of Hope* in ASJ

Dear Nick,

Let me join you in taking a broader perspective on the work of ASJ than I have taken up to this point in these letters. Let me speak about the role of hope in our pursuit of justice-in-shalom in Honduras. It's my conviction that our hopefulness sets us apart from other organizations and people working in Honduras, and that it is a crucial part of our success.

A few months ago, I spoke with a journalist about the progress we are seeing in Honduras. She incorporated my hopeful quotes into a story with the gruesome title, "Bloody Honduras," illustrated by a photo of a masked gang member holding a gun—not the message I was trying to get across!

I commonly see this trend in reports about Honduras. Publications still refer to Honduras as the "murder capital of the world," six years after homicides dropped enough for it to relinquish that title. In fact, in 2018, Honduras' two largest cities had dropped out of the top thirty most violent cities in the world. Notably, two US cities, Saint Louis and Baltimore, still made that list. Yet politicians and policy experts shrug off advances in Honduras, and write about the situation here as "hopeless."

Honduras does face serious problems. Although poverty and homicide rates have dropped significantly, they are both far too high. Drug trafficking and corruption rot political structures in Honduras from the inside out. In our advocacy work, hard-earned wins can be overturned by capricious laws or political stonewalling.

Nonetheless, we hold tight to the fact that not only can Honduras improve, it already has. In important and meaningful ways, as I've written, the Honduras of today is different from the Honduras I moved to in the 1980s. In recent years, the homicide rate has dropped by more than 50 percent, dozens of drug traffickers have been extradited, more than $1.5 billion of assets have been seized back from criminals, and major corruption cases have been made public and resulted in arrests.

Honduras isn't hopeless, and its people haven't given up hope either. I think about my neighbors, who despite poverty and difficult living situations, still hold on to dreams for their children and for their own future. They work hard, sacrificing so their children can study, build extra rooms on their homes, and start new business ventures. If they can envision a brighter future for themselves and take active steps toward it, why shouldn't I?

A Long View of Change

At ASJ, we believe that change is possible, partly because we've already seen it. We have been fortunate enough to see dramatic results from our efforts over these twenty years. We ourselves have grown from a small coalition of friends to an organization with a national voice and more than 150 employees. But I don't think our victories can totally explain our hope. Instead, I believe that hope contributes to the sustaining of our work—not vice versa. We ran ASJ for years without seeing dramatic growth or nation-wide successes, trusting that our work was building on itself and that in time we would see results.

In 2009, when many children spent more days out of school than in; in 2012, when Honduran homicide rates peaked; in 2016, when the depth of police corruption was revealed, we didn't let these overwhelming challenges dishearten us but instead redoubled our efforts. I think it was this hope in spite of circumstances that allowed us to see the transformation we have seen.

Shane Claiborne and John M. Perkins write about this long view of transformation in their book *Follow Me to Freedom*. Claiborne writes:

> [John Perkins] came down to visit our little experiment in community on the north side of Philadelphia ... I remember later that day whining to John about how we had been working so hard and hadn't seen much of anything get better. There were still gunshots all the time—there was still heroin, there was still complaining.
>
> "It's been over three years and there aren't many signs of change," [I said]. John looked me dead in the eye and, with the gentleness of a father, plainly and so sincerely explained the way things work:
>
> "Oh, Shane, *you'll start to see some things change. You'll start to see signs of transformation—in about 10 years. Or maybe 12.*" And he didn't flinch. That was his promise: we'd see change *in 10 or 12 years.* I gulped. That was nearly half my life up to that moment, yet somehow I knew he spoke the truth, and it gave me hope.

When I read this book, ASJ was around fourteen years old. I thought back, and realized that it was exactly in that time frame, ten to twelve years, that we had begun to see a shift in our credibility and impact. Our work in education helped to ensure that, in 2011, all children received 200 days of class for the first time. Our work in violence helped tip the scale and, by 2014, homicides were dropping sharply. In 2018, thanks to our work reforming the police, more than 5,000 corrupt officers had been purged from the police force. Our hopefulness and dedication have fueled these fragile successes, which have built on each other over fourteen years of work. The longer we commit ourselves in a single place, the more we see the effect of our work cascade and grow.

We've held on to this "ten-year rule." We're in Honduras for the long haul, which changes the scope of what we hope for. We're not trying to get a victory before finishing a two-year placement, or ending a three-year grant. I'm satisfied even if our work is pushing us closer to victories that could take a decade to be fully appreciated.

Celebrating Small Changes

While ASJ is by character hopeful, we certainly do go through periods of feeling overwhelmed or discouraged by how much work remains to be done. But still we manage to hold on to hope. In addition to taking the long view of change, another way we stay hopeful is by recognizing and celebrating individual improvements, however small they may be.

Ever since ASJ was a very young organization with only a few staff, we dreamed big and thought about how we could lead significant changes in Honduras. But we didn't start with those giant goals. We broke them down into smaller manageable pieces, which allowed us to recognize when we were getting closer to a big goal, even if we weren't there yet. This wasn't a matter of debating whether the glass was half-full or half-empty; this was a matter of celebrating those first few drops at the bottom of the glass.

When we got land titles for one community, we barely put a dent in the hundreds of thousands of untitled plots of land across the country. However, we helped to change the lives of 100 families, and what's more, we also learned important lessons about how the system worked, building experience for a future overhaul of the Honduran Property Institute. When we won a case guaranteeing the minimum wage for a group of fifty security guards, we knew that as many as 74,950 guards were still waiting for their turn. However, we were making a substantial difference in the lives of these guards and their families, while also opening scrutiny of unjust hiring practices that would ripple out and become a broader movement.

Each victory fills the glass a little more. As we are helping individuals, we are also gaining information, building networks, growing in respect and legitimacy with other organizations and authorities, and improving our ability to tackle bigger problems in the future. Not only is this a hopeful way of looking at our slow and steady progress, it's a practical one. If we had started in 1998 by trying to reform the police force, without putting in the years of building up the knowledge and credibility that would eventually make that possible, we would have failed miserably, and probably would have been discouraged from trying again.

Calling

Our understanding of our Christian calling is another important part of what sustains us. We believe that God has called us to transform Honduras and that God will give us the strength and wisdom to do it. God also promises that we are not in this work alone or even responsible for its success. The Holy Spirit is the agent ushering in and pointing to the kingdom and invites us to be part of that transformation.

I can think of so many times when we felt that we were at the end of our rope or boxed into a corner. In each of those moments, I believe God broke in with a new idea or a change in circumstances that allowed us to move forward. We have never been left out to dry for long. This has been an encouragement for us, that we are on the path God desires for us. If we felt called to do this work, and put in the effort but saw no openness, no results, no transformation, then I think we would eventually need to question our calling. I don't believe God calls people to failure. That doesn't mean results come quickly or easily, but it does mean that if you are faithful in your kingdom work, you will eventually begin to see evidence of God's kingdom.

ASJ faced a particularly challenging time in 2009, when President Mel Zelaya was ousted in a coup. People in the country divided along party lines and over whether they were for or against the coup. Confidence in public institutions tanked. There were widespread protests. In the aftermath of this, we gathered a group of organizations together to try to harness all that negative energy and turn it in a positive direction. We agreed that regardless of politics, fixing the broken education and health systems had to be priorities for government and civil society—and the resulting coalition, Transformemos Honduras, would become a leader in precisely those issues. We didn't see transformation right away, we saw it after years of gathering evidence, presenting proposals, and consistently seeking God's calling.

Our belief that we can, and should, do something about such deep division and serious issues can seem naïve to others, especially in the face of everything we are up against. I am sure there have been occasions when our hope has led us to be taken advantage of, when our good-faith efforts were twisted or abused. Still, I would always rather err on the side of trust and of trying than let fear keep us from intervening in an area where we could have made a significant difference.

I never want to be afraid of big ideas. People laughed at and dismissed our broad vision when we started ASJ. Twenty-one years later, we continue to get the same criticism. Imagine if we had waited until public opinion was on our side. We never would have started.

Healthy Dissatisfaction

Of course, faithfulness can't consist of sitting around and waiting for success to come to you. I don't think "wait on the Lord" means sitting on your hands. For this reason, ASJ has sought to cultivate an organizational culture of what I think of as healthy dissatisfaction.

A few years ago, Andrés Oppenheimer, a respected journalist and writer on Latin American policy, came to speak in Honduras and joined ASJ for a presentation on the state of education in the country. Oppenheimer has traveled all over the world to study education policy. He said that in Latin America and Europe, education leaders put a lot of stock in their long history—their country's traditions and what they have done in the past. China and India, by contrast, have a very different attitude. When it came to education policy, they were perfectly happy to throw the past out the window as long as it improved their outlook in the present. What's more, the two countries had a sharp eye out on each other; they were competitive in their policies, adapting innovations that seemed to be working in the other country, always working to outpace each other.

The researcher found that while Latin American and European scores were stagnant, this competitiveness has helped China and India earn huge gains in the quality of their public education. They are now on track to join the educational epicenters of the world.

I like to think that ASJ fits that model too. We're perpetually dissatisfied with the way things have always been done, or with the common knowledge of how civil society or religious organizations are supposed to work. We're curious about what others are doing, always adapting and evolving, always tweaking our approach to stay one step ahead of the corrupt politicians or business leaders who are trying to game the system. We lose battles, and that can frustrate us; but it also motivates us to try even harder.

Historically, for example, the church has been silent on issues of politics and corruption in Honduras, preferring to speak out only on moral issues within a narrow range that didn't step on any toes. One of our most recent programs, "Brave Christians," breaks with that paradigm, seeking to mobilize the church, especially young Christians, around issues of justice and transparency. During the recent election process for a new Attorney General, we mobilized thousands of believers to pray over the process, appearing on television, radio, and in large prayer meetings to preach the importance of accountable government systems.

We may face criticism for stepping out of what people feel is the purview of nonprofits or church groups, but we're also connecting with people, especially young Christians who may have felt previously that they had to make a choice between their faith and their activism. Not only that: politicians are taking note. The Attorney General may have met with these young Christians right after his election because Protestants make up over 50 percent of Hondurans and are an important demographic. A few weeks later, however, when pressure and threats against him had increased, he was the one who called us asking for prayer.

We're not afraid to break new ground ourselves, but we're also fascinated by strategies and innovations that have worked around the world. Honduras is in desperate need of electoral reform, and since the lead-ups to the 2017 election, we have been speaking out about reforms to make Honduran democracy more transparent, representative, and just. We recently hosted a conference together with the Carter Center in the United States where we heard from experts about the experiences of electoral reform in Mexico, the Dominican

Republic, and Ecuador. Mexico is much bigger than Honduras, Ecuador is much richer, the Dominican Republic has a different history and context—but while we understand that their solutions would need to be adapted for Honduras, we don't write off their experience as irrelevant. We aren't satisfied with sticking to the status quo.

A Good Team

All four of the reasons for hope that I mentioned—our long view of change, our ability to recognize and appreciate small changes, our feeling of being called to this work, and a healthy dissatisfaction with the status quo—are essential to avoid burnout and hold on to hope; but none of it would be possible if we did not have such a phenomenal staff who shared these ideas.

"If you want to change the world," my friend and colleague Omar Rivera often says, "you'd better have a really good *team*." He means that you need to choose well the people who will surround you, people who think as you do and who share your values, people who are competent, motivated, and just as hopeful as you are that change is possible. We are fortunate enough to have a staff at ASJ that meets every one of those criteria.

I could fill an entire letter just singing the praises of our staff: my co-founder and friend Carlos Hernández, and Omar Rivera, who tirelessly leads our advocacy work and also serves on the police purge commission. I could talk about the police homicide-chief turned ASJ investigator, the former public prosecutor now helping us combat child sexual abuse, the legal expert who has ghostwritten dozens of Honduran laws, and so many other women and men who spend their days sharing hope in communities. I hope the next time you visit us you can meet many of these people in person.

Your friend,
Kurt

PART 4

ASJ AS A CHRISTIAN ORGANIZATION

23

In What Way Is ASJ a Christian Organization?

Dear Kurt,

Most of my letters have been quite long. This one is going to be short—very short!

Hovering in the background of our discussion has been the fact that ASJ is a Christian organization. Though you and I have both alluded to this dimension of ASJ, we have not, up to this point, made it a topic of discussion in its own right. Organizations are Christian in many different ways. Before we bring this exchange of letters to a close, I would like you to explain in what way ASJ is a Christian organization. Being a Christian organization obviously does not mean, in your case, that you work only with other Christian organizations. In your discussion of how ASJ works, you noted that ASJ cooperates with a wide range of organizations, including secular organizations. So in what ways does being a Christian organization make a difference in how you in ASJ think and work—a difference in your goals, your strategies, the alliances you form, your conduct?

Your friend,
Nick

24

ASJ and Its Staff Seek to Act
in a Way that Is a Testimony to Jesus

Dear Nick,

You bring up a very important point, namely, our identity as a Christian organization. ASJ works on issues like governance, anticorruption, and violence—areas that few Christian organizations tackle. So we regularly receive questions about what influence, if any, our Christian identity plays in our work. What exactly do we mean when we say that ASJ is a Christian organization? If you scrubbed the Bible verses from our webpage or skipped our all-staff devotional meetings, would anything else set us apart? But you are right: since the beginning, our vision has been bringing about God's desire for shalom in Honduras.

Transparency International (TI) is the world's leading anticorruption organization. In 2012, they invited us to join their network of anti-corruption organizations; we were officially accredited as a National TI Chapter in 2015. Recently, TI's president José Ugaz visited us, and told us that out of TI's more than one hundred chapters, ASJ was one of the three "star" chapters he held up as an example of positive anti-corruption work around the world.

Few of TI's national chapters are Christian organizations. Some people in the TI network cite our Christian commitment as an explanation for our good work. As Christians, they say, we must be motivated by higher goals, making us bolder in speaking out in unpopular or controversial ways.

I have heard this said by Christian speakers and authors as well—that Christian organizations can be identified by the superior quality of their work. People suggest, by way of explanation, that Christian organizations care more, love deeper, and may even see God intervening on their behalf to ensure that their initiatives prosper.

This would be a neat explanation, but unfortunately, it doesn't ring true to me. It implies that non-faith-based organizations will always be worse than Christian organizations—either because they love less, or because they are motivated by earthly or material motivations. This has not been my experience. What's more, over my years in this work I have come in contact with many Christian organizations doing very mediocre work, or worse, caught up in severe problems of corruption or sexual abuse. Christian principles don't always line up neatly with excellence or success.

I believe in the theological concept of common grace—the idea that God's blessing has been extended to all creation, and that God's good works can be carried out by anyone who is trying to love and be a blessing to others. Christians have no monopoly on helping others. I would argue that God is working today through organizations like Transparency International, Amnesty International, and other secular organizations that are fighting injustice around the world, despite the fact that these organizations do not consider themselves Christian, or their work to be Christian work.

Another way to examine ASJ's Christian identity would be to ask whether we evangelize or proselytize; do we use ASJ as a platform to spread Christianity? Here we enter into stickier territory. Non-Christians may like what we are doing with our anti-corruption or violence prevention programs, but be uncomfortable with the promotion of a particular religion. A focus on evangelism can raise difficult questions for Christians working in these programs.

Some Christian organizations offer benefits only to Christians, while others serve everyone but require beneficiaries to listen to a Christian message or receive Christian materials before being served. Still others offer Christian messages or materials that are optional. What is the "appropriate" level of proselytization when meeting individuals' material needs? Both as individual Christians and as leaders of a Christian organization, how should we relate the "mission" of a Christian organization as that is generally conceptualized in Christian circles (converting non-Christians to Christianity), and our organization's specific mission, which is to make Honduran government systems work more justly and does not explicitly include religious conversion?

As we at ASJ have reflected on this question, we have arrived at two goals that respond to the question above, and to the broader question about what sets us apart as a Christian organization.

First, we do see our work as directly Christian, kingdom work. Context here is important. Honduras is between 80 to 90 percent Christian, with a higher rate of church attendance than the United States. Evidence of Christianity is everywhere here, in schools, in political speeches, in graffiti on city walls and bumper stickers on public buses. The problem in Honduras is not that people have not heard of Jesus, but that they may have seen his name abused or misrepresented.

Therefore, personally and through ASJ, we seek to live our lives in a way that is a testimony to how Jesus truly lived. We want to be brave, to stand up for victims and the oppressed, and defend their rights. This model of living is attractive to people who have felt that their desire for justice was ignored by the church, or incompatible with life in the church. In multiple cases, our example has invited people to further explore what it means to be a Christian, and to see God in a new way.

When I arrived in Honduras over thirty years ago, the country was around 95 percent Catholic, with Protestants a small minority. Since then, the Protestant church has exploded, and the most recent surveys show that the current breakdown is closer to 45 percent Catholic and 45 percent Protestant, with around 10 percent claiming no religious affiliation. Despite this surge of conversions, the country still suffers from widespread corruption, income inequality, and a homicide rate that is far too high. How is this possible?

It's certainly not just a problem of the "faithless" 10 percent. Political elites attend church services on Sunday then pass a law on Monday that makes it nearly impossible to investigate corruption cases. We have even heard of pastors who accept money from drug traffickers for the purpose of building a new church, or who look the other way while drugs are stashed in the church's storeroom. Clearly, there is a disconnect between their talk and their walk.

The second aspect of our evangelism, then, is "evangelizing" those who already consider themselves to be Christians. If you look at the life of Jesus, the apostles, and the prophets, they were consistently at odds with the religious status quo. Prophets were often the lone voices daring to speak out against oppressive kings and leaders. From Moses to Nathan to Elijah to Isaiah, we see God's messengers standing up to power in defense of those who have been marginalized or oppressed. Jesus continued and perfected the tradition that came before him. He publicly challenged corrupt church leaders, overturned tables in the temple, and taught subversive messages that denounced oppressive Roman authorities while also defusing desire for a violent insurrection.

Despite all this, if you poll the average person on the street asking them which words they would use to describe Christians, almost no one would say "brave," and few would describe Christians as being on the front lines of defending those who have been oppressed. Christians are comfortable modeling Jesus' humility, compassion, and love. Why have we strayed from modeling his bravery and zeal for justice?

At ASJ, we want to evangelize the church to reclaim this aspect of their faith and to live it out, to be brave Christians focused on protecting the poor and marginalized. Therefore, at ASJ we consistently and publicly claim our Christian identity, while also unmasking corruption, working in violent and dangerous neighborhoods, and denouncing government and pressuring it to do what's right for its people. These are very high-risk, uncommon Christian pursuits. This public claiming of our faith, backed up by bold work, allows us to witness both to Christians and non-Christians, modeling an active faith that is concerned not only with people's eternal souls but also with their earthly flourishing or shalom.

Last year, we started the Brave Christians program I mentioned in letter 22. Brave Christians is staffed by church leaders who are concerned about injustice in their country, in part, a result of our years of efforts to be more intentional about challenging the way that Honduran Christians and churches live out their faith. Brave Christians leads Christians in prayer for broken government systems and for injustices from the family to the national level, while also informing them and encouraging them to join advocacy movements to address the issues they are praying over.

Through this movement, we are bringing into conversation those who are more comfortable in prayer with those who are more comfortable using their hands, voice, and power to denounce injustices—I think to the benefit of both groups. As we pray and work together, we remember in humility that it is through God's grace that we are able to do this work. This motivation, purpose, and focus is how I would define ASJ's Christian identity.

Your friend,
Kurt

25

ASJ Enacts Fundamental Themes in Christian Scripture

Dear Kurt,

Thanks for answering the question I posed to you as to the way in which ASJ is a *Christian* organization. Over the years I have learned that a good many evangelical organizations doing relief or development work, when asked this question, point to the fact that the staff assembles on a regular basis for prayer and devotions and engages in various forms of evangelistic activity. That is not what you pointed to. Your staff does in fact assemble on a regular basis for prayer and devotions. I know, because I have been present at some of those assemblies; my wife, Claire, has, on occasion, led them. But that's not what you point to. You point to the fact that the way in which ASJ and its staff *conduct themselves* has an "evangelizing" or "witnessing" function. "We seek," you say, "to live our lives in a way that is a testimony to how Jesus lived. We want to be brave, to stand up for victims and the oppressed, and defend their rights." You observe that this is a witness both to those outside the church "who have felt that their desire for justice was ignored by the church, or incompatible with life in the church," and to those inside the church who assume that Christianity is only about "people's eternal souls" and not about "their earthly well-being."

Let me take this discussion about ASJ as a Christian organization a bit further. I would say that, in addition to the witnessing function you point to, ASJ is a Christian organization by virtue of intentionally enacting some fundamental themes of Christian (and Hebrew) Scripture. Let me identify three of those themes, in each case taking a bit of time to establish that the theme is indeed fundamental in Scripture.

Social justice, the sort of justice that is the primary concern of ASJ, is one of those fundamental themes. In Isaiah 61:8 we read, "I, the LORD, love justice." In Psalm 37:28 we read, "The LORD loves justice." These are just two of dozens of passages, perhaps hundreds, that declare that God loves justice.

To understand what Scripture is saying, when it declares that God loves justice, we must keep in mind the distinction I drew in previous letters between first-order and second-order justice. If one thinks of second-order criminal justice when one reads that God loves justice, one will assume that what the biblical writers mean, when they say that God loves justice, is that God loves the imposition of punishment on those who "offend against God's holy laws."

I submit that if one pays attention to context, it becomes clear that when Scripture declares that God loves justice, almost always the sort of justice in view is first-order justice. God also loves a well-functioning criminal justice system, the reason being that first-order justice in our world is constantly under threat in the absence of a well-functioning criminal justice system. But criminal justice is *for the sake* of first-order justice; it's not for its own sake. First-order justice is basic.

One form that God's love of justice takes is that God calls you and me, and all our fellow human beings, to love and seek justice. We are called to participate in God's cause of loving and doing justice. In a well-known passage from the Old Testament book of Amos (5:24) God says, "Let justice roll down like waters, and right-doing like an ever-flowing stream." And in an equally well-known passage from the Old Testament book of Micah (6:8), the prophet says,

God has told you, O mortal, what is good;
and what does the LORD require of you
but to do justice, to love kindness,
and to walk humbly with your God.

Just as I could quote many more passages than the two quoted above, in which we read that God loves justice, so too I could quote many more than these two in which we read that God enjoins human beings to love and seek justice.

In its pursuit of social justice, ASJ is enacting the biblical theme that God loves justice and enjoins us to participate in God's work of loving and pursuing justice.

From the words and deeds of ASJ we learn that, in its struggle for social justice in Honduras, it gives priority to the fate of the little ones, the marginalized, the downtrodden. People of wealth and power are also sometimes the victims of social injustice. But as you wrote in one of your previous letters, ASJ wants "to stand up for the victims and the oppressed, and defend their rights." I submit that, in giving priority to the fate of "the victims and the oppressed," ASJ is enacting a second fundamental theme in Christian Scripture.

A striking feature of what Scripture says about justice is that, over and over, the presence or absence of justice in society is connected to the fate of the widows, the orphans, the aliens, and the impoverished. Here is Isaiah speaking:

> Seek justice,
> rescue the oppressed,
> defend the orphan,
> plead for the widow. (1:17)

A few chapters later we read:

> Woe to those who decree iniquitous decrees,
> and the writers who keep writing oppression,
> to turn aside the needy from justice
> and to rob the poor of my people of their right,
> that widows may be their spoil,
> and that they may make the fatherless their prey.
>
> (10:1–2)

From the dozens of passages I could cite in which the same point is made, let me add just one more, this one from the Psalms:

Give justice to the weak and the orphan;
maintain the right of the lowly and the destitute.
Rescue the weak and the needy;
deliver them from the hand of the wicked. (82: 3–4)

The connection that the biblical writers draw between justice and injustice, on the one hand, and the fate of the widows, the orphans, the aliens, and the impoverished, on the other hand, is so unusual and striking that one is bound to ask, what does it mean? How are we to understand it?

A commonplace among the South American liberation theologians who were writing in the 1960s and 1970s was that what is coming to expression here is what they called God's "preferential option for the poor." This suggestion infuriated a good many well-to-do North American Christians. "What do you mean, God's preferential option for the poor? Doesn't God love everybody equally, rich and poor alike? You don't have to be poor to be loved by God."

My response is: true, God does love one and all. Nonetheless, there's no getting around the fact that when the biblical writers declare that God loves justice and enjoins us to do so as well, over and over the widows, the orphans, the aliens, and the impoverished are mentioned.

Once again, why? Why this persistent emphasis on what one might call "the quartet of the vulnerable"? Let me offer a suggestion.

When we work for social justice, we have to set priorities. Powerful and wealthy people do on occasion get mugged, burglarized, and so forth. They too are the victims of injustice—the victims of *episodes* of injustice. But compare their situation to that of the widows, the orphans, the aliens, and the impoverished in old Israel. These were the vulnerable ones; they had no power or wealth. Their *daily condition* was a condition of injustice and of threats of injustice. Yes, they too would have suffered *episodes* of injustice: muggings, for example. But they were vulnerable to *the condition of their daily existence* being unjust.

If we are seeking social justice, we have to deal with those who are victims of *episodes* of injustice. But our priority has to be those whose *daily condition* is unjust. That's why there is, in Scripture, a preferential option for the quartet of the vulnerable. In its work, ASJ enacts this fundamental theme of Scripture.

There is a third theme in Christian scripture that ASJ seeks to enact. As I have remarked several times in these letters, what struck me on my first visit to ASJ, and again on all my subsequent visits, is the implicit assumption in everything it does that it is the task of the Honduran government to secure justice in Honduras. And as I argued in an earlier letter (#5) this is exactly what Christian Scripture says is the task of government in general.

In the way it works for social justice in Honduras, ASJ enacts the biblical theme, that it is the God-given task of government to secure justice in society. ASJ does not content itself with dispensing aid and charity to victims of injustice. Nor does it content itself with issuing denunciations of injustice. Neither does it try to do an end run around government. It holds government officials responsible for securing justice, and it aids them in doing so.

ASJ is a Christian organization in the way that you emphasize, Kurt, namely, by the organization and its staff conducting themselves as a "testimony to how Jesus lived," a testimony both to those within the church and to those outside. But it is also a Christian organization in the way that I have highlighted in this letter: it seeks to enact—to actualize—some fundamental themes in Christian Scripture.

Your friend,
Nick

26

A Question about Christians and Social Justice

Dear Nick,

I'm glad that you see evidence of our Christian faith in ASJ's work. It's one thing for us to claim that we are a Christian organization; it's another thing for observers to say that they discern evidence of that identity.

I'm going to follow your example and make this letter short. In your letter, you quote many different passages to support your understanding of justice in scripture, in particular, the prioritizing of first-order justice over criminal or second-order justice. Your examples are compelling; but they go against the current of a lot of present-day Christian discourse. While many North American Christians are perfectly fine with criminal justice, they are quite wary of any call for social justice.

In our conversations with each other, we discussed this wariness and resistance; and you mentioned that you attributed it, in part, at least, to a certain misreading or misinterpretation of the Bible. What is that misinterpretation? The idea that a concern for social justice would be thought not to be biblical is hard for me to understand.

Your friend,
Kurt

27

Explaining Social Justice, and Noting Its Importance in Scripture

Dear Kurt,

Let me preface my answer to your question about the role of justice in Christian Scripture by explaining what I take social justice to be, something I have not done up to this point.

I understand social justice to be a special version or type of first-order justice. As I explained earlier: first-order justice is present in society insofar as we treat each other justly in our ordinary relations with each other—shopkeepers and clients treating each other justly, teachers and students treating each other justly, parents and children treating each other justly, etc. Social justice pertains not to individual cases of first-order justice but to the laws, regulations, and practices of a society. It's present in a society when, in following its laws, regulations, and social practices, the individual and institutional members of society treat each other justly. ASJ is primarily a social justice organization. As you have noted several times, it deals, for the most part, not with individual cases of just or unjust treatment but with the laws, regulations, and social practices of Honduran society. To use a word you have employed several times, its concerns are "systemic."

When social justice is understood along these lines, there are, quite obviously, two potential sources of social injustice. The laws, regulations, or practices might be unjust; that is, they might require citizens and institutions to act in ways that are unjust. Or the laws, regulations, and practices might be just, but citizens and institutions might be violating those requirements.

What are customarily called *social justice movements* are movements to diminish or eliminate some form of social injustice. If a movement identifies the source of the injustice on which it has its eye to be certain unjust laws, regulations, or practices, it aims at revising those laws or regulations or at reforming those practices. Alternatively, if it identifies the source of the injustice on which it has its eye to be violations of just laws, regulations, or practices, it aims to get the individual and institutional members of society to obey those laws or regulations or to follow those practices.

The work of ASJ takes both forms, but especially the latter. In the area of education, for example, ASJ discovered that, whereas the law reasonably requires students to receive 200 days of class per year, many students were receiving no more than 125 days.

It has been the experience of both of us that a good many Christians are wary of social justice work. In my experience they are usually not wary of *criminal* justice. It's endeavors to secure *social* justice that they are wary of. And what I have learned, from discussing this wariness with them, is that very often the source of their wariness is a certain way of interpreting Christian Scripture. There are other sources of wariness. But in this letter, let me focus on their interpretation of Scripture as a source of their wariness.

What I have learned is that a good many Christians believe that in the New Testament, first-order justice, and especially first-order *social justice*, has been superseded by love. First-order justice, they think, is obsolete Old Testament stuff. They don't think second-order criminal justice is obsolete. They continue to be in favor of prisons and jails; and many of them attribute a desire for retributive justice to God and believe that that has to be satisfied. But they think that love, not justice, should govern our ordinary relations with each other. They recognize that, over and over, the Old Testament declares that God loves justice and enjoins the Israelites to do so as well. But the New Testament, so they say, enjoins love instead.

Let me mention two considerations that encourage this interpretation of the New Testament. First, in the Sermon on the Mount, Jesus said that we are to love our neighbors as ourselves; he did not say that we are to treat our neighbors justly. And in his farewell address to his disciples, as recorded in the Gospel of John, Jesus says, "Love one another, as I have loved you." Again, no mention of treating each other justly. It appears that love has supplanted justice.

But has it? That depends on what Jesus meant by "love." The word in the Greek original of the New Testament that is translated into English as "love" is *agapē*. A common interpretation of the meaning of *agapē*—probably *the most* common—is that *agapē* is *sheer gratuitous benevolence*: seeking the good of the other person out of sheer gratuitousness, not because it is required of one.

Treating other persons justly is required of one; it's not an option. So if the love that Jesus enjoined is understood as sheer gratuitous benevolence, then love and justice are pitted against each other.

But is that what Jesus meant by love (*agapē*)? Well, when Jesus gave the so-called second love command in the Sermon on the Mount, he was not just stating the essence of the Torah in response to a critical questioner; he was actually quoting from the Torah, specifically, Leviticus 19:18. So, to understand what Jesus meant by love of neighbor, the relevant thing to do, obviously, is look at the occurrence of the love command in Leviticus to see whether the context in which it occurs there illuminates the meaning. What we find when we look at that section of the book of Leviticus is a rather long list of quite specific injunctions to the people of Israel as to how they are to treat each other and those who sojourn among them, that long list concluding with the injunction, "Love your neighbor as yourself." The injunction to love your neighbor as yourself is the summary of what has preceded. And among the injunctions that precede the love command are injunctions to the people of Israel to treat each other justly, both in their ordinary interactions with each other and in how they treat wrongdoers.

The conclusion is unavoidable, that the sort of love Jesus had in mind when he said that we are to love our neighbors as ourselves does not supersede justice but incorporates justice. Loving one's neighbor as oneself requires, as a minimum, that one treat one's neighbor justly. Loving one's neighbor often goes beyond what justice requires; but it never falls short of doing what justice requires.

I said that there are two considerations that encourage the view that justice is superseded in the New Testament by love—love being understood as sheer gratuitous benevolence. Let me move on to the second consideration. This consideration applies to those who read the New Testament in an English translation, not to those who read it in a translation into one of the Latinate languages: Spanish, French, Italian, Portuguese, etc. Whereas the word *justice* often occurs in English translations of the Old Testament, in most English translations of the New Testament it seldom occurs.

The Greek adjective *dikaios* and the Greek noun *dikaiosunē* occur hundreds of times in the original Greek text of the New Testament. When these words occur in classical Greek texts—Plato, Aristotle, etc.—they are almost always translated into English as "just" and "justice." In most English translations of the New Testament, they are instead translated as "righteous" and "righteousness."

Why this change in translation? It's possible, of course, that in the roughly three hundred years between the classical Greek writings and the New Testament, the meaning of the terms *dikaios* and *dikaiosunē* changed from "just" and "justice" to "righteous" and "righteousness." However, an indication that our New Testament translators don't think the meanings changed completely is the fact that, in a few passages, they do translate the Greek words as "just" and "justice," and the fact that a few translators (especially those of the original *Jerusalem Bible*) regularly translate them as "just" and "justice." My own view is that, in Greek of the New Testament time, the terms had become somewhat ambiguous. Sometimes *dikaiosunē* meant *justice*; sometimes it meant, more vaguely, *doing the right thing*. Context has to determine how we translate the terms into contemporary English.

I am assuming that, in contemporary English, "righteous" does not mean the same as "just" and that "righteousness" does not mean the same as "justice." It matters how we translate. "Righteousness," in present-day English, names a character trait of individuals. A righteous person is a person of upright character, a person of rectitude. When used in religious contexts, "righteous" and "righteousness" often connote piety: an upright person is a pious person. "Justice," on the other hand, names a social relationship. Justice pertains to how we treat each other, how we act toward each other.

The thing to do at this point is to take a Greek New Testament in one hand, an English translation in the other hand, find a place where *dikaios* is translated as "righteous" or *dikaiosunē* as "righteousness," look at the context, and judge whether the New Testament writer was talking about righteousness or about justice. I judge that very often the context makes clear that the writer was not talking about the personal character trait of righteousness but about acting justly or rightly. Here I limit myself to just two examples.

In the Sermon on the Mount Jesus says, "Blessed are those who are persecuted for the sake of *dikaiosunē*" (Matthew 5:10). Most English translations read, "Blessed are those who are persecuted for the sake of righteousness." I submit that this makes no sense. People are seldom persecuted because they are righteous; righteous people are typically either admired or ignored. It's people who struggle for justice that are persecuted. They get under people's skin. The staff of ASJ knows this all too well!

In the same sermon Jesus says, "Blessed are those who hunger and thirst for *dikaiosunē*." Most English translations read, "Blessed are those who hunger and thirst for righteousness." Is that a plausible translation? Do people hunger and thirst for a righteous character? Isn't it more plausible to interpret what is being said as that people hunger and thirst for justice in society?

Here's an exercise that anyone can perform. Almost always in English translations of the New Testament, the words "righteous" and "righteousness" are translations of the Greek words *dikaios* and *dikaiosunē*. When you come across "righteous" or "righteousness" in an English translation, consider the context, and ask yourself whether the writer is talking about the character trait of rectitude or about acting justly or rightly. Employ this exercise, for example, on what was traditionally called the parable of the Great Assize in Matthew 25, now often called the parable of the Sheep and the Goats, where, in verses 37 and 46, the words "righteous" occur in most English translations, noticing, while doing so, that almost all the actions that Jesus cites as done by the *dikaios* person are cited in the book of Isaiah as acts of justice.

In short, by virtue of how the Greek words *dikaios* and *dikaiosunē* are translated, almost all contemporary English translations of the New

Testament convey to readers the message that the New Testament is about personal righteousness, of which love is a central component, not about justice. Because contemporary English translations of the Old Testament speak often about justice, our contemporary English translations of the New Testament convey the message that the New Testament is discontinuous, in this respect, with the Old Testament. It's my view, to the contrary, that it is impossible to understand the message of the New Testament in general, and of the ministry of Jesus in particular, without bringing justice into the picture.

This last point, concerning the ministry of Jesus, could be developed at length (in my book *Justice: Rights and Wrongs*, I devote two chapters to the topic). Here I limit myself to just a couple of considerations.

In the fourth chapter of his Gospel, Luke tells the story of what happened when Jesus attended synagogue one Sabbath in his home village of Nazareth. Jesus was invited to read Scripture, and was handed the scroll of the Old Testament book of Isaiah. He opened the scroll and spoke these words:

> The Spirit of the Lord is upon me,
> because he has anointed me
> to bring good news to the poor.
> He has sent me to proclaim release to the captives
> and recovery of sight to the blind,
> to let the oppressed go free,
> to proclaim the year of the Lord's favor.

Jesus then sat down and said, "Today this scripture has been fulfilled in your hearing." He was thereby identifying himself as the Lord's anointed of whom Isaiah had spoken.

When we look up the extended passage in the book of Isaiah from which Jesus read these verses, and similar passages in other parts of the book of Isaiah, we learn that the prophet explicitly says that the one who acts in the way described is doing justice. Jesus' self-description of his ministry is that he has been anointed to bring about God's reign of justice.

When the Apostle Peter, after Jesus' crucifixion and resurrection, delivered a public speech in which he reproached the crowd for having rejected Jesus, he called Jesus "the holy and *dikaios* one" (Acts 3:14). And in the speech that Stephen gave at his martyrdom, he too called Jesus "the *dikaios* one" (Acts 7:52). Jesus is the just one whose mission it is to inaugurate God's realm of justice.

The New Testament does not reject the Old Testament theme of justice. It gives that theme new content. Pull justice out, and everything falls apart.

Your friend,
Nick

28

Understanding Christians' Indifference
to Social Justice Work

Dear Nick,

You build a compelling case for social justice being a fundamental theme in Scripture, both Old and New Testaments, and for our giving priority, in the struggle for social justice, to those you refer to as the "quartet of the vulnerable"—widows, orphans, those who are foreign, and those who are poor. It is encouraging for me to read these points stated so clearly and concisely. Though I was raised in the church and attended Christian schools, I wasn't exposed to these ideas until much later.

After I had begun to see the centrality of the theme of justice in Scripture, I spent years complaining about the indifference or resistance of Christians to justice. I had the sense that the church in general—both in Honduras and in the United States—was turning a blind eye to the justice issues that seemed so important.

I do see something of an awakening in the US church today, interestingly, much of it being led by young people. Justice issues like sex trafficking and the death penalty are gaining traction within church circles, and conferences about justice are increasingly common.

However, a lot of this still appears to me more talk than action. I worry that the focus is still, too often, "over there" instead of within the US itself. It's hard to reconcile those glossy, packed-stadium conferences with the deeply entrenched racism, broken school systems, and street-level violence in the cities around them. There are, of course, Christian leaders who are addressing these challenges—I think of John M. Perkins' work with the Christian Community Development Association in Mississippi, and Bryan Stevenson's Equal Justice Initiative. I'm sure you could name many more individuals who are making a difference in local justice issues. Despite some notable exceptions, however, I think that the church is still not leading change for the majority of issues that most affect the poor and vulnerable in the United States.

I also see some signs that the church is awakening here in Honduras. Pastor Alberto Solórzano, head of the coalition of evangelical churches, and probably the most prominent Protestant leader in Honduras, used to be quite resistant to the idea that Christians should have anything to do with politics. But after seeing members of his congregation suffer from crime and corruption, and getting involved in the work of ASJ, Solórzano has become an outspoken voice for government transparency, and was even named to the Commission to purge the Honduran National Police alongside other ASJ staff and board members.

We have seen several other religious leaders in Honduras find their voice for justice in the public sphere—our board includes the director of the Church of God and the national director of World Vision, and they have joined us in speaking out on difficult issues like corruption in public education. You would not have seen this openness and forthrightness a few decades ago.

So today I do see in some ways less direct resistance to social justice work from the global church; but I do still see a lot of misunderstandings of what exactly social justice looks like, or how we can get involved to create change.

One troubling trend I see is the Christian tendency to let good intentions excuse weak implementation. A youth group in North America decides they want to "do justice" in the world, so they build a school for children in Honduras—but none of them has experience managing a construction project, none of them understands the country's educational context, none of them has done the due diligence required to analyze whether their intervention is appropriate or helpful for the population they're trying to reach. In the end, because of their lack of experience and understanding, this youth group is not going to be very effective.

Effective justice work looks very different. Effective work directly challenges those who misuse their power for personal gain. This is off the radar for many religious groups. Few people who go to build a well in Africa ask questions about why the local Secretary of Infrastructure was unable to provide the water.

When you ask those difficult questions, when you touch powerful interests, people get angry; people fight back. To really, effectively work toward the justice and shalom that we are called to seek, I think we as Christians need to do the hard work of preparation, of gathering evidence, determining underlying root causes of the problem, and determining practical proposals to address those root causes rather than just the symptoms that show how something deeper is broken.

When we at ASJ grew frustrated that children were leaving school still unable to read, we dug in and asked the hard questions. When we discovered that schools were only meeting 125 days per year, we understood that was a symptom of corrupt politicians and teachers' unions that didn't have the best interests of children in mind.

When we saw our neighbors suffer from a lack of medicines at public hospitals, we started an investigation that ultimately uncovered exactly how unscrupulous people were using the medicines warehouse as a personal piggy bank.

Our work in violence asked even more difficult questions about what was corrupting the police force, and which laws and systems were giving drug traffickers free rein.

Our hearts may have pulled us into these areas—we at ASJ care deeply about the education, health, and safety of the people in Honduras—but to move forward, we needed to use our minds, and commission expert research and diagnoses.

I also think we need to be open to allowing this evidence to change our expectations of how our churches should serve. If research finds that food banks, water projects, or twelve-step programs are not the most effective way to combat the issues we care about, we need to be open to other options, especially those that go deeper into structural and systemic injustices.

I speak from time to time at churches in the United States, and I find them filled with very skilled, insightful business leaders, accountants, teachers, and innovators. There's no reason why they should leave their talents at the door. We should expect as much rigor and excellence from our mission programs as we expect from our companies' performance.

What's more, the church has a great deal of credibility to speak about these issues—more than one might think. The commission to purge the Honduran police force was made up of pastors and Christian leaders, alongside lawyers and politicians, which gave the process greater legitimacy in the eyes of the public. It was clear that we were doing this not out of personal interest but out of a desire to improve our country.

Ultimately, justice work becomes an extension of sharing the gospel. As an organization, ASJ has frequently entered spaces where we are the only voices speaking from a place of faith and religious devotion. We aren't evangelizing in the street—but politicians ask us for prayers. We don't lead religious services, but ambassadors or foreign officials are drawn to us and ask us about the faith they see in us. This vision of a faith that seeks action, a religion that is based on justice—this is compelling for many people, and can even draw them back to the church they had lost faith in.

I think justice can also be compelling to people within the church; but they may need more exposure to these ideas, and they may need an express invitation to participate.

Bob Laarman, director of Disaster Response Services for World Renew, the development agency Jo Ann and I worked with when we first came down to Honduras, once observed that when he worked with communities of people living in poverty, his inclination was to be patient and understand that changing practices or patterns of thinking wasn't something that would happen overnight. Why, he challenged us, do we think it's easier for groups or congregations in the United States to change their habits? When working with the church in the United States, we should have a similar long-term outlook and investment of time.

Of course, this may require those of us who self-identify as "justice advocates" to revisit our own attitudes concerning spreading our message. Instead of coming to churches with criticism, feeling we have all the answers, and wanting to change their minds so that they think like us—we should approach them from a posture of personal relationship and mutual learning.

When we come to groups of Christians, not with attacks but with invitations and opportunities, we see tremendous growth in the area of justice. Pastor Solórzano changed within a few years, from someone who was skeptical of the church doing justice work, to taking on leadership at another anti-corruption nonprofit that has joined with ASJ on several of our transparency initiatives.

I see this as another important part of ASJ's work. Through our work we are not only providing a Christian example to people outside the church but "re-evangelizing" the church itself—showing people who care deeply about their faith that they can express it publicly and make a difference in the lives of many. It has never been our intention to lead this work alone; we want to invite the church to join us, and ultimately we want to walk alongside them as we do this work together. I think we are beginning to see that movement.

Your friend,
Kurt

29

The Uniquely American Christian Resistance
to Social Justice Work

Dear Kurt,

My experience of recent years parallels yours. After I was awakened to the importance of social justice by the two experiences in the late '70s that I described in my second letter, I began to give talks about the nature and importance of justice to groups of Christians. The audiences were always small, twenty or thirty people—there was very little interest in the subject.

In 2011, I was invited to speak at a conference on justice that was sponsored by an organization that called itself simply "The Justice Conference." The conference was held in Bend, Oregon, not a major population hub. To my utter amazement, there were 1,100 people in attendance, most of them in their twenties or early thirties. Since that initial conference, The Justice Conference has sponsored biennial conferences at which the attendance has been over 2,000. Something is stirring.

I have heard some people downplay this development by saying it's just another youthful fad. For those young people with whom I had conversations at these conferences, it was clearly not a fad; they were serious and committed. But even if it were a fad, there are fads much worse than this one!

Not only were the groups small when I first began speaking about justice. Invariably there was resistance to what I was saying. Initially, this resistance puzzled me. Before my awakenings, I had not noticed how prominent in Christian Scripture is the theme of justice. Now it jumped out. Over and over God declares "I love justice," and over

155

and over God asks of you and me that we share that love. I pointed this out to my listeners, quoting a few passages. I could understand that the theme of justice in Scripture had previously not caught their attention, just as it had not caught mine. But once I pointed out how prominent it is, how could they resist?

I could understand resistance if I had accused people in the audience of being perpetrators of injustice. Who likes being the subject of an accusation? But I had not done that. My examples were almost always things I had learned from my reading about the situation in South Africa and in Israel/Palestine. Injustice off in the distance!

Gradually I began to understand. It turned out that one source of resistance was the conviction that justice has been supplanted by love and righteousness in the New Testament, a conviction that I addressed in my last letter. Another source of resistance proved to be the connection I drew between justice and rights; I became aware of the fact that a good many of my listeners were intensely averse to rights-talk. I also discussed this source of resistance in a previous letter.

Every now and then yet another source of resistance to what I was saying surfaced in the questions put to me, this one peculiarly North American. Nothing peculiarly North American about the preceding two sources of resistance. I was told that justice is a liberal idea. Initially, I was dumbfounded. Why would anyone think that justice was a liberal idea? Were Amos and Isaiah liberals?!

What I eventually concluded was that, in some quarters of North American Protestant Christianity, especially evangelical quarters, there is a lingering cultural memory of the social gospel movement, a movement of theological liberals in the early decades of the twentieth century that emphasized the importance of social justice. In the minds of many, both those who supported the movement and those who opposed it, theological liberalism and a concern for social justice became associated with each other. I was amazed to find that there remained, in some quarters, a lingering cultural memory of that association. I had assumed, without thinking about it, that that memory had long ago faded away. Probably I should not have been amazed. Deep habits of thought get passed on from generation to generation.

When those whose thinking was shaped by a cultural memory of the social gospel movement told me that justice was a liberal idea, what they had in mind was that it is a *theologically* liberal idea. I have recently been awakened to the fact that some of those who told me that justice is a liberal idea probably had *political* rather than *theological* liberalism in mind—or perhaps both. What awakened me to this possibility was reading a recent (2014) publication by Benjamin T. Lynerd, *Republican Theology: The Civil Religion of American Evangelicals.* In his book, Lynerd traces what he calls "evangelical political theology" over the past two centuries. One of his contentions, supported by multiple quotations, is that a persistent component in American evangelical political theology is the pair: individual liberty and limited government. Several times in these letters I have observed that Scripture teaches that the God-given task of government is to secure justice in society. The American evangelical political theology that Lynerd traces says nothing about its being the task of government to secure justice. What it says instead is that the task of government is to secure individual liberty, and that to do that, it must remain small.

I think we can safely infer that some of those who say that justice is a liberal idea have political liberalism in mind. When they hear the term "social justice," they think of big government, and they associate big government with liberal politics.

How have I dealt with the charge that justice is a liberal idea? If it is Christians who are making the charge, I have done my best to make clear that social justice is foundational to Scripture. It's not a liberal idea. It's a biblical idea!

And now I have a question for you, Kurt. In the course of my letters, I have highlighted some of what I see as the distinctives of the work of ASJ. ASJ starts from those who are victims, more specifically, from those who are wronged by some action or inaction on the part of the government, not from those who are victims of natural disasters or personal folly. And ASJ doesn't then just call out a few corrupt or ineffective officials (though it does do that on occasion) but it deals with the government agency that is failing—the police force, the educational system, the health system, etc.—with the aim of prodding and enabling the agency to serve the cause of justice.

ASJ is so clear in its focus and so distinctive in its way of working, and its steady work over the years is now proving so effective, that one naturally wonders whether the ASJ model can be employed by people in other countries who are working for justice. ASJ did not begin with some big general ideas, devised in some think tank, about how to reform society in general, and then try to apply those general ideas to the Honduran situation. Its work throughout has been crafted to the particularities of the Honduran situation. And that raises the question: Can the work of ASJ be a model for similar work in other places? The work of ASJ evokes admiration, stirs the imagination, suggests possibilities. But can it also serve as a model for justice work elsewhere?

Your friend,
Nick

PART 5

APPLYING THE ASJ MODEL ELSEWHERE

30

Applying the ASJ Model
to Police Reform in Chicago

Dear Nick,

You ask a good question. We have been asked many times about replication of our work elsewhere. We are very clear that despite the general mandate to do justice, there is no cookie cutter approach to carrying out that mandate. Each particular situation of injustice is a result of specific dynamics that can't be generalized. But I think over the past few years we have come to identify certain patterns and principles. I want to share one example of an occasion when we worked with a US organization to try to share, as you call it, the "ASJ model."

After we at ASJ became involved in efforts to purge and reform the Honduran police, we were drawn into conversations about best practices in policing ranging from Colombia and Chile to Canada and the United States. In one of those conversations, I learned that while Honduras has one national police force, the United States has over 18,000 separate forces, making it very difficult to advocate for systemic reform. In addition, police chiefs, generally hired at a city level, have a great deal of power in their position. Many of them come into the force with their own ideas of how things should be run, and are quick to scrap past chiefs' projects for their own idea of what works. In a world where we increasingly face structural rather than localized threats to our safety and well-being, having these atomized police forces, driven by very individualistic police chiefs, makes reform difficult.

Nonetheless, to answer your question, I do believe that ASJ's work—and especially our work in police reform—can be a model elsewhere. Naturally, our work cannot be replicated exactly in other contexts. However, I believe that the ASJ model is transferrable, to some extent, and that our key ideas can work in many countries.

There was a group of business and nonprofit leaders in Chicago, for example, who came down to observe our work in Honduras. In 2017, they invited us to visit Chicago to advise them on how they might be able to combat violence in the city. We learned there that although Chicago was around the same size as New York City or Los Angeles, and rates of poverty were similar in the three cities, violence in Chicago was much worse.

Looking at these numbers, it is clear that there is something happening in Chicago—something beyond quick social or environmental answers people might offer. It seems that the policing is at least part of the reason why.

The Chicago police force has faced many scandals for corruption or brutality. There have been attempts at reform; but the police unions have been very resistant. Almost no systemic changes have been made, and almost no officers have been fired.

While our friends in Chicago were open to hearing about our experience, they were initially very skeptical of the idea that something similar to our police reform work could be done there. They talked about the strong unions, about the decentralization, and about geographic factors, focusing on all the ways that Chicago is different from Honduras.

I understood their points. I grew up on Chicago's South Side before the area became synonymous with rampant crime and gun violence. But as I worked on turning the tide of violence in my Honduran neighborhood, I became convinced that the underlying issues—corruption, weak systems, and injustice—weren't too different from the place where I grew up.

We told the group in Chicago that to work for reducing homicides and violence, they would have to start with good data and solid statistical analysis. This would allow them to identify root causes of violence, and to support the bold and controversial claims they might have to make. Once they had these numbers in hand, they would need to find a way to make them public, probably through the national media. This requires steadfastness and bravery, because it is not easy to criticize public institutions with a long-established history and a high PR budget. However, despite the risks, reports by civil society can have a lot of credibility with the public, especially when these public institutions have so obviously failed the public. Finally, we told them, once the information is public they would need to commit to keeping the statistics in the public eye, pressuring government systems until they begin to change.

As we broke our philosophy down to these key elements, it began to seem evident that any challenges unique to Chicago could be overcome. Furthermore, if our methodology had worked in Honduras, a country with weak systems and scarce funding, it could certainly work in Chicago, a city with twenty-five times the GDP of Honduras and substantially more stable courts and public systems.

It took a few hours and a lot more examples, but by the end of our conversation, the group was convinced not only that they could do something similar in Chicago but that they should.

This has been our experience in other places as well. In places ranging from a land rights conference in Brazil to a Transparency International summit in Berlin, people are interested in the model of change that we have developed. And through these conversations and exchanges, we have learned that much of what we do in Honduras is transferrable. It needs adjustment to different contexts and issues, but in the end, we often find ourselves realizing that social problems are human constructions, and that we humans are not as different from each other as we might think.

An "ASJ-inspired" program in the US, or in El Salvador or in Thailand would look different because cultures and social problems vary in real and important ways. But our goal isn't replication of our programs as much as adaptation. What we really want is to share our core ideas—so we talk about gathering good evidence, taking it public through the media, being willing to walk alongside government authorities, holding them accountable, and helping them to implement change. The more we dig into these core ideas with people around the world, the more we hear them say, "Well, maybe ..."

They start to realize that by tweaking this and adjusting that, these programs just might work.

Now I'd like to ask you to elaborate on something that came up in one of recent conversations and that I think is an important issue to tie in to our discussion on injustice. You mentioned that a fundamental cause of injustice in the United States today is populism. I would find it very helpful if you would define populism and elaborate on how, as you see it, populism leads to injustice.

Your friend,
Kurt

31

Populism and Its Challenge to Justice

Dear Kurt,

You asked me to explain how I understand populism. At the core of all present-day populist movements, as I understand them, is lament over loss, or the threat of loss, specifically, over the loss or threatened loss of a way of life. In the US, it's lament over the loss of a way of life in which men had good jobs in factories and mines, in which the population was generally Christian, in which one's neighbors were of European origin, in which every able-bodied man worked and none was on welfare, in which women were housewives, in which there were no same-sex marriages, in which the regulatory state barely existed. The list goes on and on. In other countries, the list is somewhat different. In Europe, the list typically includes lament over the loss of national autonomy to Brussels. Yet, the similarity of the lists for different countries is striking.

Often the more specific losses are bundled together into one big loss: the loss of the American way of life, of the Dutch way of life, of the French way of life. A report in the *New York Times* of April 21, 2017, has Marine le Pen asking, at a rally of her supporters, "Will we be able to live much longer as French people in France," to which the audience chanted in response, "This is our home!" At another rally she asked, "Do we defend the [French] nation or is the nation finished" (*New York Times*, April 16, 2017).

It's the lament for loss that makes populist movements significantly different from nationalist movements. Afrikaner nationalism was not aimed at recovering a lost way of life but at seizing power from the British and establishing a new way of life for Afrikaners, a way of life in which they had hegemony in an ethnically and racially pluralistic society. So too, liberation movements and rights movements, such as the American civil rights movement, are not aimed at recovering a lost way of life but at achieving a new way of life.

The loss that members of populist movements lament almost always includes economic loss. That accounts for the fact that the active members of these movements are mostly members of the middle class. The rich are economic winners rather than losers in the new situation; and the poor never did enjoy the economic well-being whose loss the middle class is now lamenting.

The populist is convinced that the loss he laments is not the result of impersonal forces about which nothing can be done. To the contrary: he is convinced that the loss is the result of action or inaction on the part of the elites in his country who hold the levers of powers in their hands and could prevent the loss. Thus the lament over loss is accompanied by anger and resentment. This anger and resentment typically has a dual focus: anger and resentment at the elites whom he identifies as responsible for permitting the loss, and anger and resentment at those groups who are instrumental in the loss: anger and resentment at immigrants for taking away jobs (every present-day populist movement is an anti-immigrant movement), anger and resentment at Muslims for diluting the Christian ethos of the country, anger and resentment at African Americans for (supposedly) being lazy and swelling the welfare rolls, anger and resentment at women for upsetting the traditional role of men in society.

The anger and resentment of the populist at the elites thought to be responsible for the destruction of his way of life typically spreads to suspicion, if not resentment, of intellectual elites: scientific elites who tell him that human beings are causing climate change, medical elites who tell him that vaccines are safe, economic elites who tell him that free trade is a good thing, etc. Claims to expertise are dismissed as a hoax.

There's a theme that unites the different foci of anger and resentment, namely, the theme of anger and resentment at legally enforced equality of treatment: at immigrants receiving equal treatment with citizens, Muslims with Christians, people of color with whites, women with men.

Incidentally, another indication of the fact that populist movements are different from nationalist movements is the resentment, in populist movements, of the ordinary people against their elites. In nationalist movements, the people and their elite leaders are united. Nationalists movements unite the leaders with their followers, populist movements divide.

It's because of anger and resentment against the groups perceived to be instrumental in the loss of a way of life that populist movements take on tones that opponents perceive as nativist, racist, and religiously prejudiced. The populist rejects the charge. He insists that he is not prejudiced against Mexicans, against Arabs, against Muslims. He just doesn't want them streaming into his country and destroying his way of life. And as for those African Americans who are citizens of the US: he's not prejudiced against them. He just doesn't want them living off welfare and threatening white people.

Be that as it may, the actions of populists mirror those of racists, of nativists, of sexists, of the religiously prejudiced.

It's important to add that the populist believes he or she has a right to the preservation of a way of life. Populists see themselves and their fellows as being wronged, as victims of injustice. Their cause is righteous. What's happening isn't fair. In short, populists perceive their movement—ironically—as a movement for social justice! The first of the *Times* articles to which I referred quotes a woman who attended one of Le Pen's rallies as saying, "I cry for my Provence. I feel hatred. By what right do they take over my country?"

It's easy for those of us who are not members of a populist movement to overlook this moral dimension of populism. Our paradigm of a social justice movement is the American civil rights movement. Populist movements are so different from the civil rights movement that they don't look to us like social justice movements. We interpret them as nothing other than expressions of anger and resentment.

I submit that they are, in fact, fed by a deep sense of moral grievance, and that we overlook this at our peril. If they were fed by nothing other than anger and resentment, we could say, "Get over it." But, fed as they are by a deep sense of moral grievance, we have no choice but to engage with them in moral dialogue—difficult as that is when one's dialogue partner is angry and resentful.

What adds to the sense of moral grievance on the part of the populists is that they perceive the elites in their country as deaf to their claim of victimhood—or worse, as ridiculing their claim. The elites listen to the claims of unjust treatment made by women. They listen to the claims of unjust treatment made by gay people. They listen to the claims of unjust treatment made by African Americans. But they are deaf to the claims of unjust treatment made by those who see their familiar way of life being destroyed. Worse yet: the elites arrogantly and condescendingly dismiss the populists making these claims as "deplorables"—in the words of Hillary Clinton. The first of the *Times* article to which I referred quoted another person who attended one of Le Pen's rallies as saying, "There are some [immigrants] who are good. But then there are others. And now they have more rights than we do."

The goal of every populist movement is to recover what was lost—in the words of Donald Trump's campaign motto, to "make America great again." Note the word "again." America was once great, America has lost its greatness, so let us band together to recover America's greatness. Critics insist that recovering our former way of life is impossible; we have to move on. The dynamics of globalization are such that jobs in manufacturing lost to countries with cheaper labor markets will never return to the US. The populist doesn't believe it. He doesn't believe in the supposedly ineluctable dynamics of globalization. He believes that the political and economic elite in his country are responsible for the loss of his way of life. He rallies around a leader who persuades him that, if given the reins of power, he will restore the lost way of life. That leader, ironically, is almost always a member of one of the elites under attack.

If the core of populism consisted of a set of policy proposals concerning the best way forward, the populist might be willing to engage in serious discussion with those presently in power who have different views on policy, and he might be willing to reach some sort of compromise. But that is not the core of populism. Its core, so I have suggested, is not policy proposals but moral grievance over the loss of a way of life, and moral resentment and anger at those identified as responsible for the loss. Its goal is to topple the elite and seize power, with the aim of restoring the lost way of life. If that is one's aim, what room is there for rational discussion and compromise? None. "You have not listened to us; why should we listen to you? Our way or no way." All populist movements harbor within them the threat of violence and authoritarianism. Before the last US presidential election, Trump declared that, if he lost, it would be because the election was rigged, and he predicted that there would be violence in the streets.

It's obvious, from the analysis I have proposed, that populist movements are ripe with the potential for injustice against those groups who are perceived as threatening the traditional way of life— against immigrants, against Muslims, against African Americans, against women, against the poor. Since, as I suggested, populists perceive their cause as just and righteous, it's a source of injustice that is singularly difficult to deal with. The ASJ model is not relevant, nor is any other model that I know of. When I look at countries where populism is currently strong, what I see them doing, each in their own way, is muddling through. The case to be made against the populist is that justice requires that we welcome those who are fleeing persecution and seeking asylum, that women be treated equally with men, African Americans equally with whites, Muslims with Christians, etc. But the populist doesn't want to hear that case.

Your friend,
Nick

32

Building Trust in Public Institutions

Nick,

Thank you for bringing populism into this discussion. Before reading your letter, I'm not sure I would have seen the relevance to our justice work, but I see now its many implications both for pursuing just practices and policies in a country, and for promoting the sort of social fabric that is necessary to form the sorts of civil society organizations and networks I have been describing.

The "moral grievance" of people with populist beliefs, which makes it very difficult for them to find common ground with those who do not share their beliefs, is present in Honduras as well. The suspicious and resentful attitude of many Hondurans toward government officials makes it nearly impossible for them to have productive discussions with those officials; and this makes our work more difficult because such a central part of ASJ's methodology is building up governmental integrity and capacity, so that the state can fulfill its responsibilities. I want to use this letter to highlight the dangers I see in such suspicion and resentment.

Reading the news, it seems clear that denigrating political rhetoric has become a new norm around the world. People don't just criticize politicians they disagree with; they actively vilify them.

This derision is coupled with very low levels of trust or confidence in public institutions. Only 26 percent of Hondurans report confidence in the National Congress; and in the United States, a country with fewer blatant cases of corruption, Congress's approval rating is currently just 15 percent. This isn't a fluke; it's been a decade since the US Congress's approval has even been above 30 percent

I understand the frustration of the US public with gridlock and other problems on Capitol Hill. But I don't understand the vitriolic and often personal attacks on politicians. I have personally met members of both the US House and Senate. I didn't have to agree with their politics to recognize that most of them were smart, educated, driven people who were truly interested in improving living situations for people in both the United States and Honduras. I don't think these individuals were anomalies.

I've found that in almost any environment, people's behavior tends to fall along a bell curve. There are almost always a few really honest, impeccable people, and a few truly despicable ones, but the majority fall in the middle. Those who fall in the middle of the bell curve tend to follow the crowd, making decisions on how to act based on the costs and benefits that are produced by the system, by the institutions, and by the legacy of culture and leadership. Positive change happens, then, when systems punish wrongdoing and reward ethical behavior, encouraging that pliable middle group to follow the outliers who would have behaved ethically no matter what the cost.

This bell curve analogy applies not just to public officials tempted by corruption, but to the general public as well. As long as Facebook algorithms, social groups, and political campaigns reward disrespectful personal attacks, that behavior becomes more acceptable. Certainly there are people modeling a more respectful and constructive attitude—but until we see a change in the cost-benefit structure, it's hard to imagine this civil discourse going mainstream.

A lack of civility and constructiveness in our public conversations can have serious costs. Both in Honduras and in the United States, we hear people constantly criticizing and tearing down public institutions. If our goal is to tear down and destroy government rather than build it up and improve it, we just may succeed—but may find our actions harming the very people we're aiming to help.

Living in Honduras, I know firsthand the cost of destroying public systems. The fragility or non-existence of security institutions in Honduras led to violence that peaked at 90 homicides per 100,000 (the United States' homicide rate is six per 100,000). Weak education institutions leave little recourse for communities whose schoolteachers never show up. A weakly controlled Congress passes laws that benefit wealthy elites and harm the general public.

Weak and corrupt institutions can have devastating consequences for our work. However, even when those institutions are made stronger and more effective, public mistrust can continue to cripple their ability to function. When Hondurans do not trust the police, they don't report crimes, they won't cooperate with investigations, and already difficult criminal investigations become impossible. When Hondurans lose faith in the education system, they stop believing that their participation and advocacy will ever make a difference.

One thing I've learned working with organizations and government institutions is that institutions are very fragile. Trust in these institutions can be even more so. It takes years to build up trust in an organization, all of which can be lost in an instant. Once trust is lost, it's very difficult to regain it, even if every member of the organization is replaced. We are very conscious of this at ASJ. I told my staff before the last Honduran elections that no matter which of the leading candidates won, our goal would be to work with them to build healthy, effective institutions that could strengthen Honduran schools, health centers, and rule of law. In an age of politicization and personal hatred towards politicians, this can seem a radical posture.

We have a responsibility to speak truth to power, and that often implies criticism, but it's important to be clear about our goals. When we are criticizing from a place of vindictiveness and anger, our criticisms often become personal and are unlikely to be constructive. If our goal is really to help the poorest and most vulnerable of our society, those who most rely on government services, we should be free and bold with our constructive criticism of public officials, but also be willing to work with them to help fix things if they are willing. We should want both for citizens to trust in institutions and for institutions to be deserving of that trust.

Your friend,
Kurt

33

A Closing Thought

Dear Kurt,

A theme that came through powerfully in your last letter was the fundamental importance—for good and ill—of institutions and systems in our lives. It's because ASJ has a clear-eyed recognition of their importance that most of its work has been at the "systemic" level, as you call it, rather than the individual level. I regard this as one of the most important and distinctive features of what I call "the ASJ model."

A good many people, in my experience, seldom think in terms of institutions and systems; they think in terms of individuals. Individuals are concrete; institutions and systems are abstract. Thinking in terms of institutions and systems requires a certain degree of abstract thinking, and lots of people do not naturally take to thinking abstractly. They like or dislike what some individual person has done—policeman, teacher, medical person, lawyer, whatever. They praise or blame the individual, without recognizing that the individual is functioning within an institution or system with a distinct authority structure, a distinct code of behavior, a distinct set of expectations, etc. Or they recognize, when confronted with bad behavior, that there is an institution or system in the background, but they just don't want to get into that. They denounce the individual and leave it at that. And then there are those who contend that if corrupt or irresponsible individuals are reformed, the reform of institutions and systems will take care of itself.

What ASJ learned, when it investigated educational practices in

Honduras, was that the problem was not just some lazy or corrupt individual teachers, but a corrupt system. Accordingly, in its concern for justice, ASJ worked for the reform of that system. It did not work for the moral or religious reform of individual teachers and supervisors on the assumption that their behavior could be reformed without addressing the corruption of the system.

In bringing this exchange of letters to a conclusion, let me move on to make one final point. In several of my letters, I have distinguished between what I call first-order justice and second-order justice—first-order justice being justice in our ordinary relations with each other, second-order justice consisting of the various forms of reproval that become relevant when there has been a violation of first-order justice. It's a distinction that goes all the way back to the ancient Greek philosopher Aristotle—though my terminology is different from his (he called them "distributive" justice and [in some translations] "corrective" justice). I think it is of capital importance to keep the distinction in mind; all sorts of confusions ensue if we do not.

That said, I want to note, in conclusion, that the two are intertwined. That became more clear to me than ever before on my first visit to Honduras, when sitting in that small living room listening to two women tell of the rape of their daughters, and of the police doing nothing about it until ASJ intervened, and listening to a young man tell of being shot by a gang, and of the police doing nothing about it until ASJ intervened. My engagement with Palestinians and with people of color in South Africa had led me to focus my attention on first-order justice. It was the violations of first-order justice in Palestine and South Africa that they were protesting. Now, sitting in that living room in Tegucigalpa, listening to those stories, I saw with stark clarity that violations of first-order justice become rampant in the midst of the pervasive fear and distrust produced by the absence of a just and well-working second-order criminal justice system. If violators of first-order justice are not punished, because the public fears and distrusts the criminal justice system, those violators will continue their violations. It is no accident that ASJ has been working not only for reform of the education and medical systems in Honduras, but also for the reform of the police system.

A Closing Thought

Let me say in closing, Kurt, that this exchange of letters has been, for me, both delightful and instructive. From your letters I have learned many things about the workings of ASJ that I had not picked up from my observations and from our casual conversations, and I have been prodded to think about a good many "theoretical" issues that I had never thought about before. So: thank you!

Your friend,
Nick

EPILOGUE

As I write these words, over a year has passed since Nick and I started our project of exchanging letters. In the midst of all the stress and surprises of directing our justice work in Honduras, Nick's letters became a welcome opportunity to take a step back and reflect. I came to look forward to the letters, which pushed me to think deeper, to connect distinct ideas, and to learn more about the biblical and philosophical underpinnings of the work that I've felt called to do.

As I read back through all the thoughts and ideas we exchanged, I'm struck by how our different paths have led each of us to work for justice in ways that support our gifts. Nick has used his speaking, writing, and activism to further the cause of Christian justice in countries around the world. In addition, his insight, wisdom, and philosophical authority gives us the language to describe and defend the work of those like my friend and co-director Carlos Hernández, who is publicly leading reforms in Honduras. Whatever our gifts, wherever we live, each of us can do justice. As Christians, I believe this is more than a possibility—it is both an invitation and a calling.

I hope readers come away from this exchange with the idea that doing justice can be complicated, messy, and sometimes dangerous—but also that it is possible. I've had people tell me that they don't want to get involved in all the complications of justice work—they just want to help people! They say this as if "helping others" is something simple and straightforward. Really, truly helping others, we've learned, is rarely so easy, and the impulse to do something quickly often results in more damage than support. When people talk about "helping others" as if it were something quick and easy, I get the feeling that they think justice work is complicated, hard, and it takes a very long time.

To those people, I like to say that, well, justice work is complicated. But it's not *too* complicated. It's often not as hard as we think, and we may see changes much faster than we think. When we let our doubts or fears interfere with our willingness to love fearlessly and boldly follow God's commands, we rob ourselves of the chance of being part of restoring God's kingdom on earth, confronting injustice, and making our homes better places to live.

This is why I want to close this book with a challenge—what will you do with these ideas you have just read? Will you follow the call for justice—a justice marked by excellence, compassion, and an other-worldly hope? Honduras is not a lost cause—no person or country is. Together, we can be part of constructing the kingdom of God, on earth as it is in heaven.

July, 2019   KURT VER BEEK

SIX QUESTIONS FOR DOING JUSTICE

Does it still seem too complicated or overwhelming to do justice in your own community? Maybe you feel convicted, but aren't sure where to start. The following questions are designed to help you discern where you can make a difference, and how you can ensure that your work is reaching structural or root causes of injustice.

1. Who is my neighbor?

Who are the widowed, the orphaned, and the poor in my immediate geographic vicinity, or in the spaces to which I feel a close affiliation, whether through family, ministry, or other circumstances?

2. What are the needs, hopes, and desires of my neighbors?

What are the yearnings that run deeper than surface-level needs? What are the underlying or "root" causes contributing to their frustration or suffering?

3. What are the structures and systems responsible for meeting these needs and allowing these hopes to be fulfilled?

Who is, as Nick says, "falling down on the job"? What institutions should be the target of our advocacy?

4. How can these systems be strengthened?

Beyond identifying errors and injustices in public systems, what are concrete and practical ways that we can make them more effective, more transparent, or more equitable?

5. With whom can we carry out this work?

Good works demands a good team. How can you walk alongside victims of injustice, allied organizations, churches, businesses, families, and communities to work towards a common goal?

6. How can we commit this work to God?

If there is one lesson I (Kurt) hope people take away from our experience with ASJ, it is that we do not do this work on our own strength, but through God's protection and providence. How can we ensure that our work is our witness, and that we are inviting others into Jesus' grace and example?

FURTHER READING

Books

Claiborne, Shane, and John M. Perkins, *Follow Me to Freedom: Leading and Following as an Ordinary Radical.*

Corbett, Steve, and Bryan Fikkert, *When Helping Hurts.*

Haugen, Gary, *Good News about Injustice.*

Haugen, Gary, *The Locust Effect*

Johnson, Kristen Deede, and Bethany Hanke Hoang, *The Justice Calling.*

Lynerd, Benjamin T., *Republican Theology: The Civil Religion of American Evangelicals.*

Oppenheimer, Andrés, *¡Basta de Historias!*

Stout, Jeffrey, *Blessed are the Organized: Grassroots Democracy in America.*

Wolterstorff, Nicholas, *Justice in Love.*

Wolterstorff, Nicholas, *Justice: Rights and Wrongs.*

Wolterstorff, Nicholas, *Journey Toward Justice.*

Wolterstorff, Nicholas, *Until Justice and Peace Embrace.*

Wytsma, Ken, *The Myth of Equality.*

Wytsma, Ken, *Pursuing Justice.*

Articles

Dominus, Susan, "Portraits of Reconciliation," *New York Times.*

Dye, David R., "Police Reform in Honduras: The Role of the Special Purge and Transformation Commission," the Wilson Center.

Hernández, Carlos, Kurt Ver Beek, Katerina Parsons, and Roland Hoksbergen, "For a Government that Works: ASJ's Theory of Change with a Case Study of their Work in Development," *Christian Relief, Development, and Advocacy journal* (CRDA).

Semuels, Alana, "Good School, Rich School; Bad School, Poor School: The Inequality at the Heart of America's Education System," the Atlantic.

Ver Beek, Kurt, "The Impact of Short-Term Missions: A Case Study of Honduras after Hurricane Mitch," Missiology: An *International Review.*

Ver Beek, Kurt. "Lessons from the sapling: Review of quantitative research on short-term missions," *Effective Engagement in Short-Term Missions: Doing it Right!,* edited by Robert Priest, William Carey Library, pp. 469–96.

Ver Beek, Kurt, "A More Perfect Love," PRISM.

Wolterstorff, Nicholas, "Just Demands: Hondurans Fight to Make Government Work," *the Christian Century.*

Other

Ver Beek, Kurt, "Reframing Justice: Models from Honduras," *January Series* lecture 2016.

Van Engen, Jo Ann, Kurt Ver Beek, David Livermore, and Lisa Van Engen, "Changed for Life Short Term Mission Curriculum," AJS Website: www.ajs-us.org.

NAME AND SUBJECT INDEX

SCRIPTURE INDEX

CPSIA information can be obtained
at www.ICGtesting.com
Printed in the USA
FSHW012059150221
78656FS